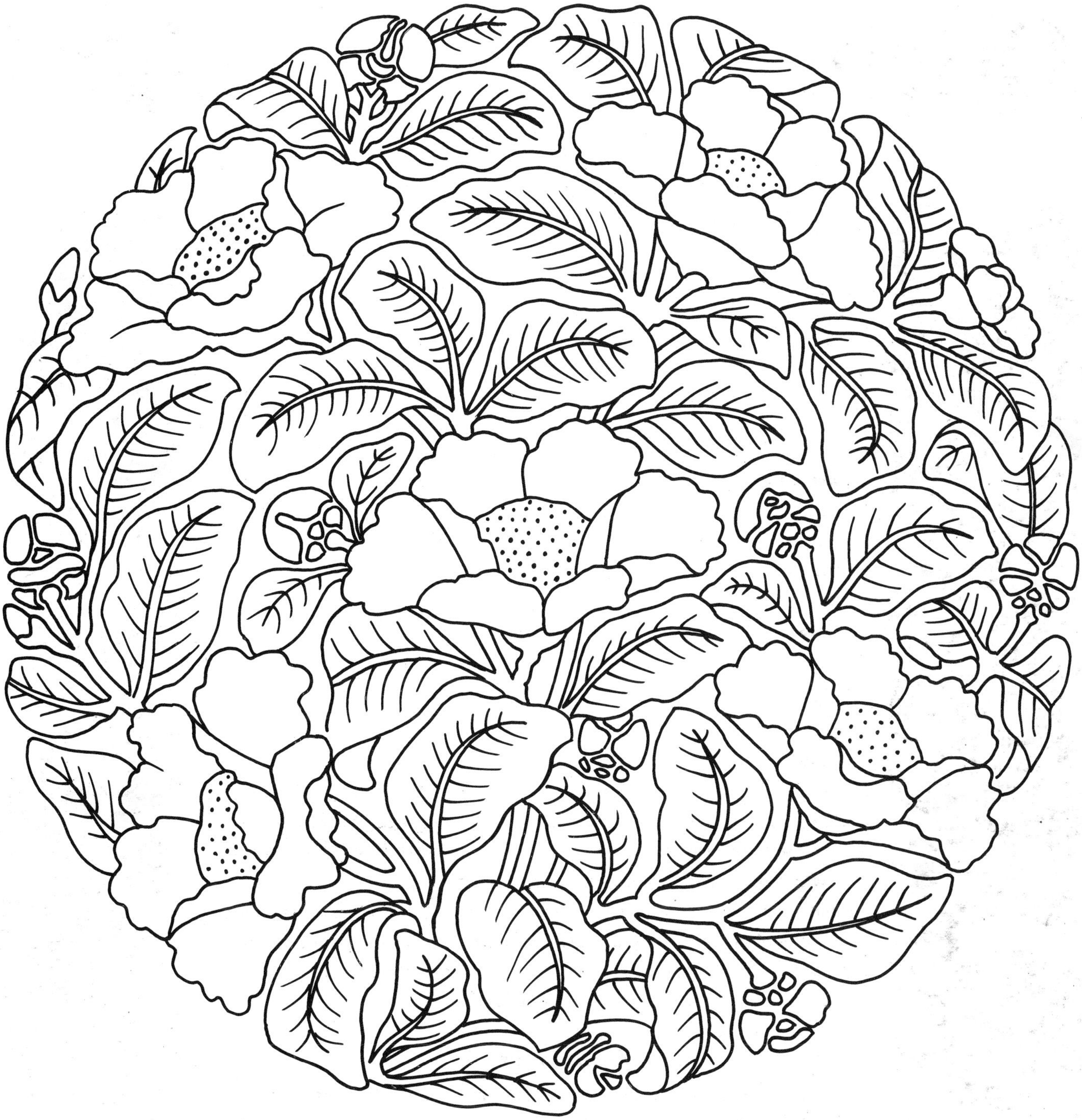

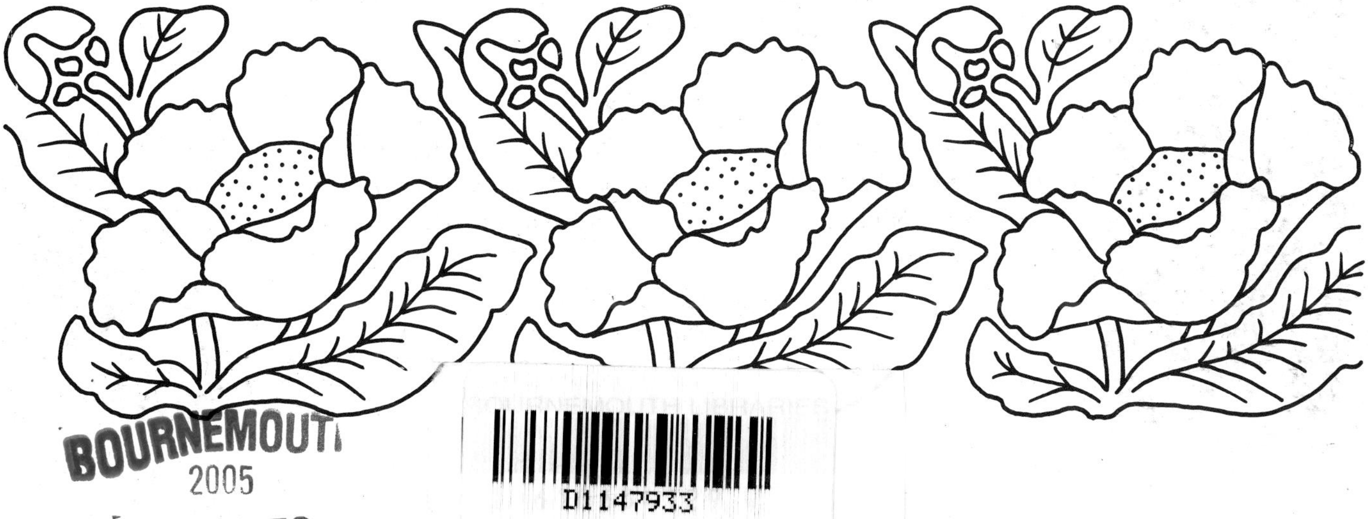

BOURNEMOUTH
2005
LIBRARIES
D1147933

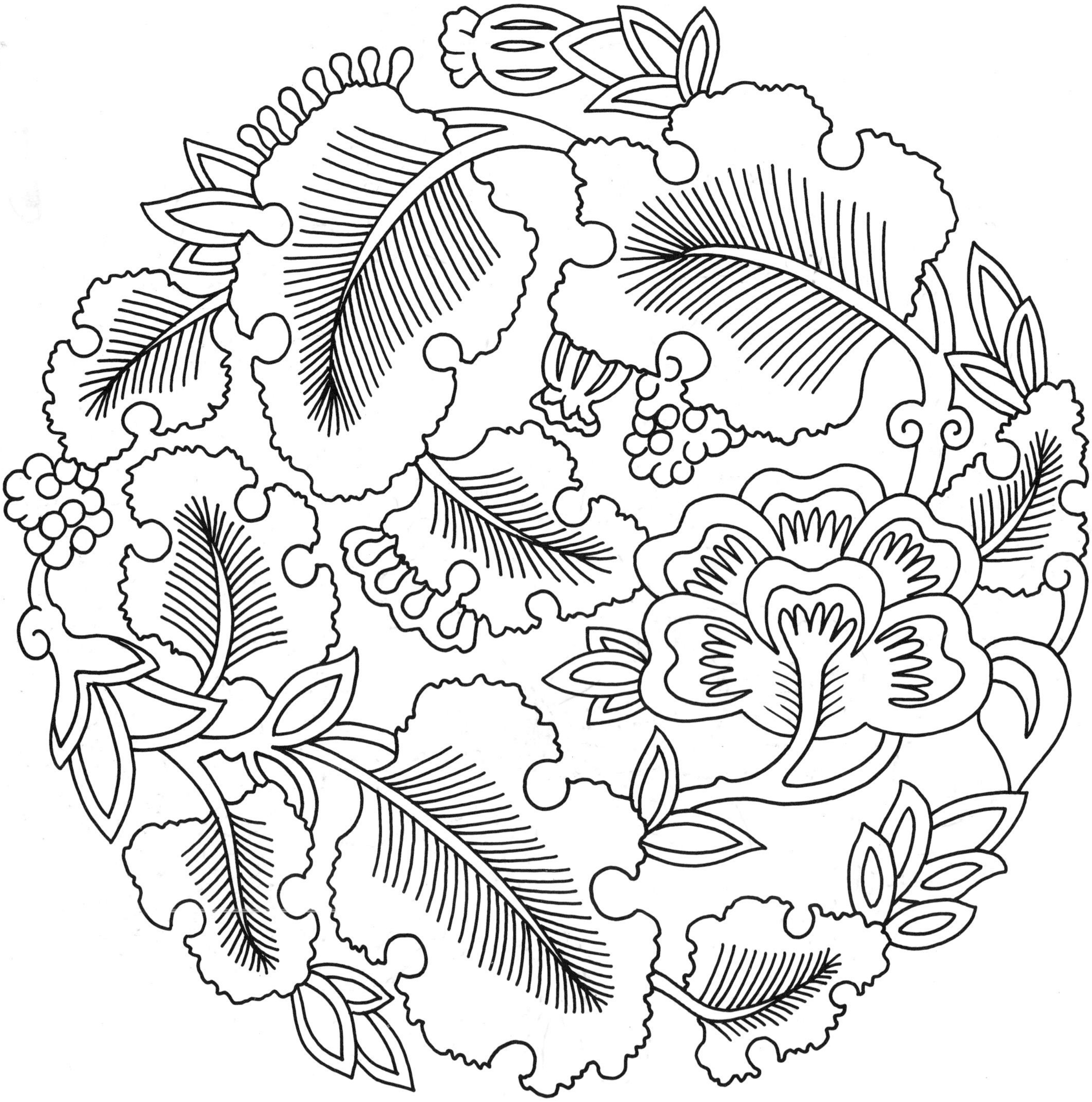

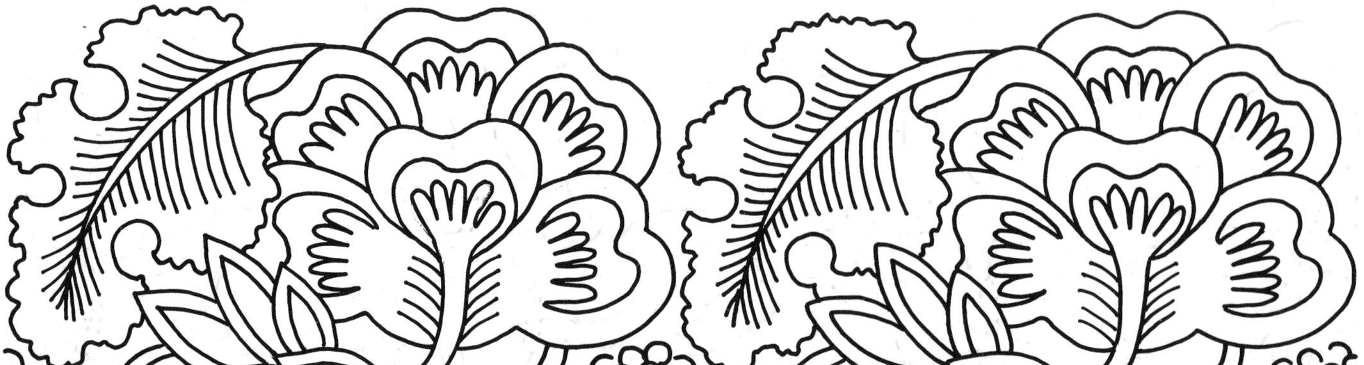

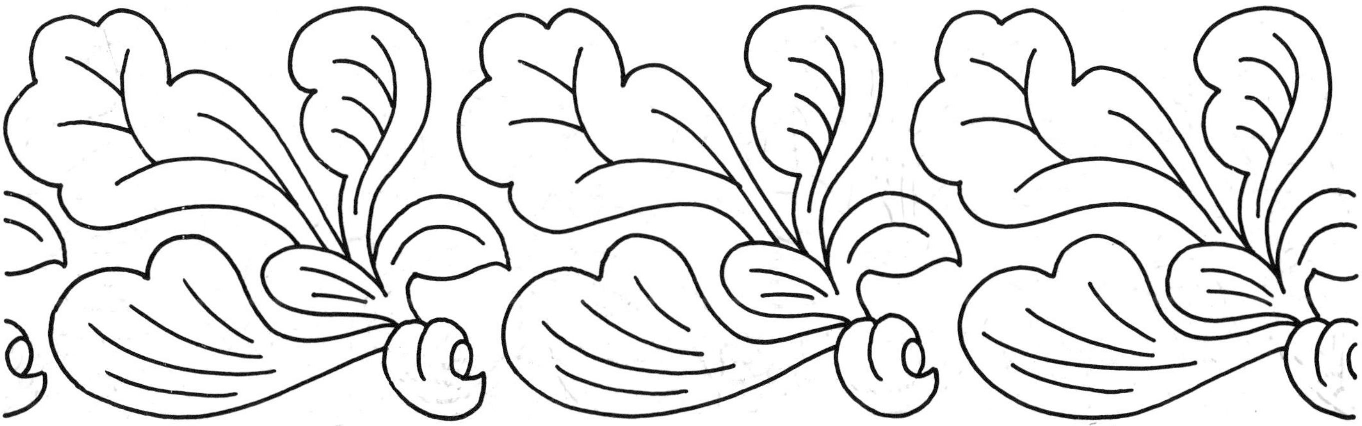

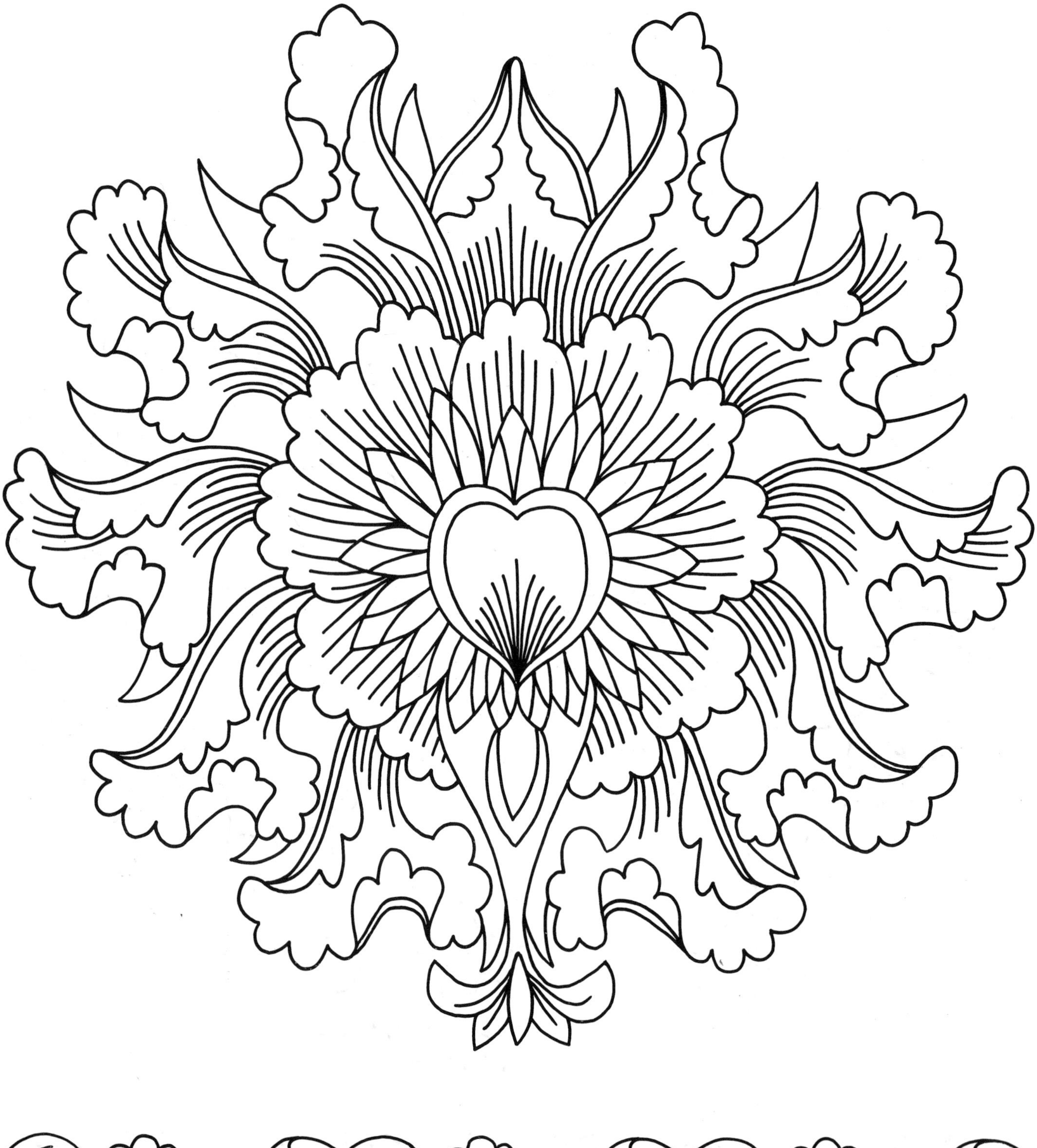
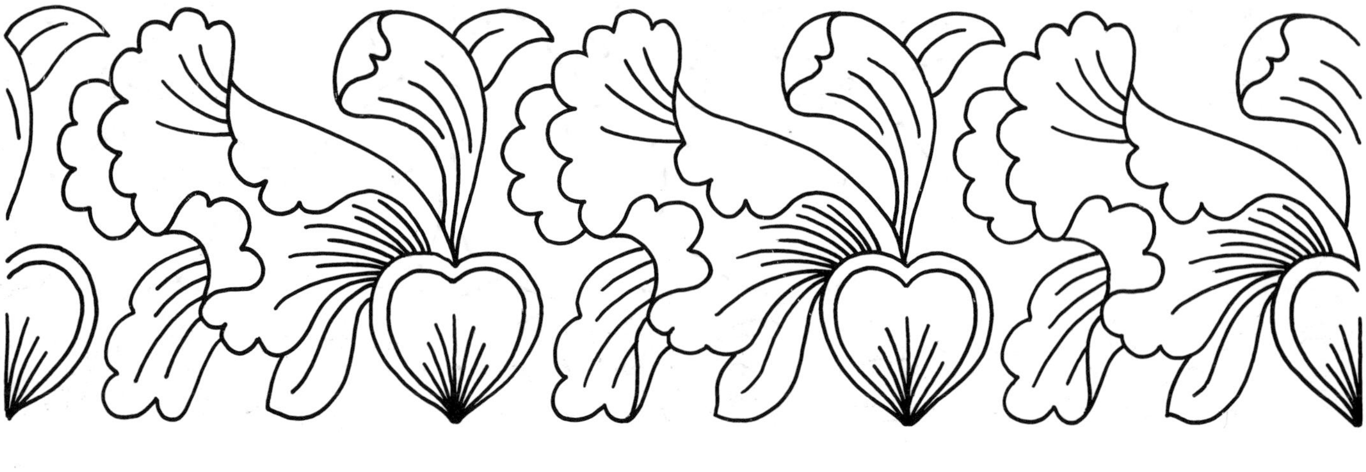

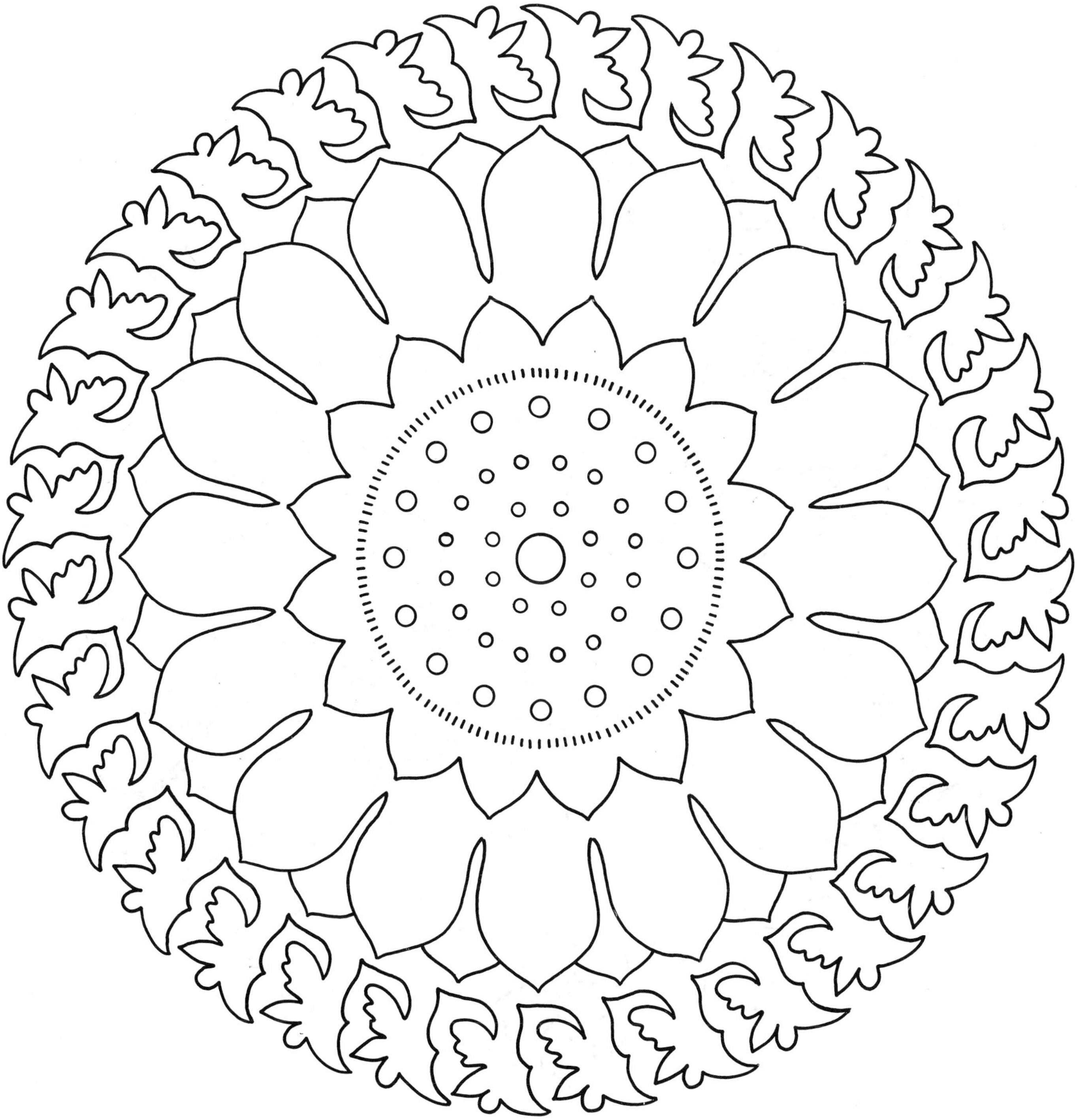
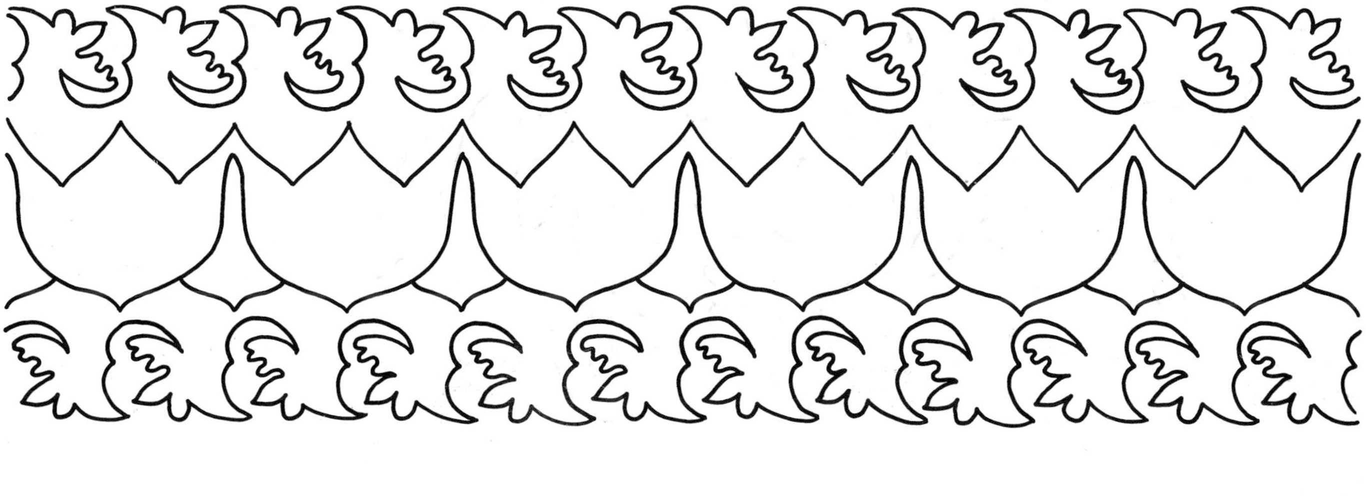

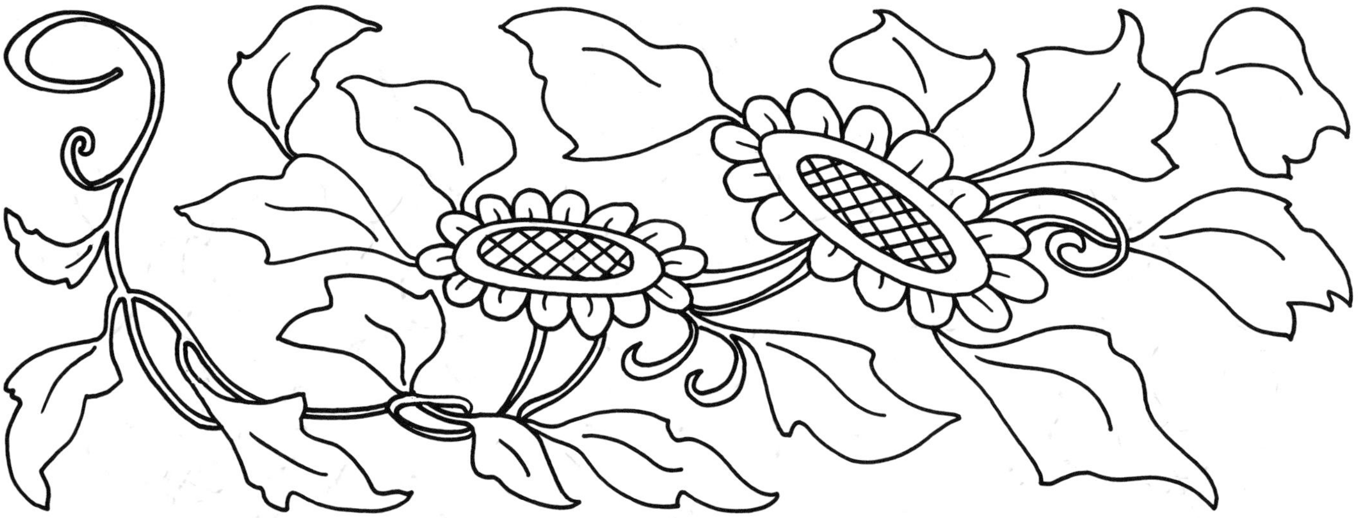

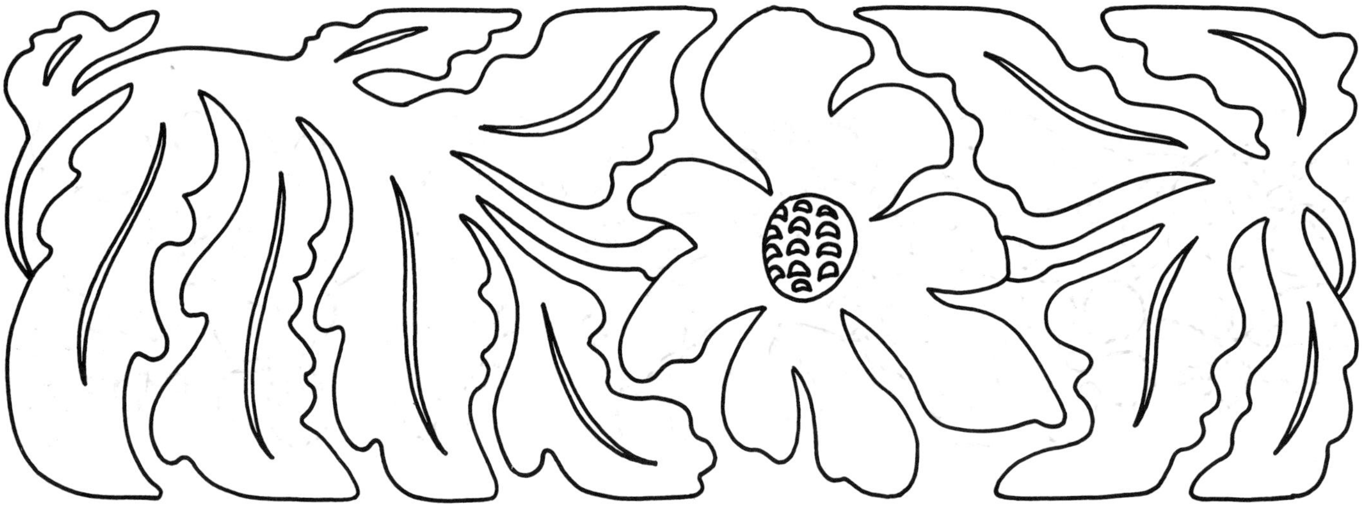

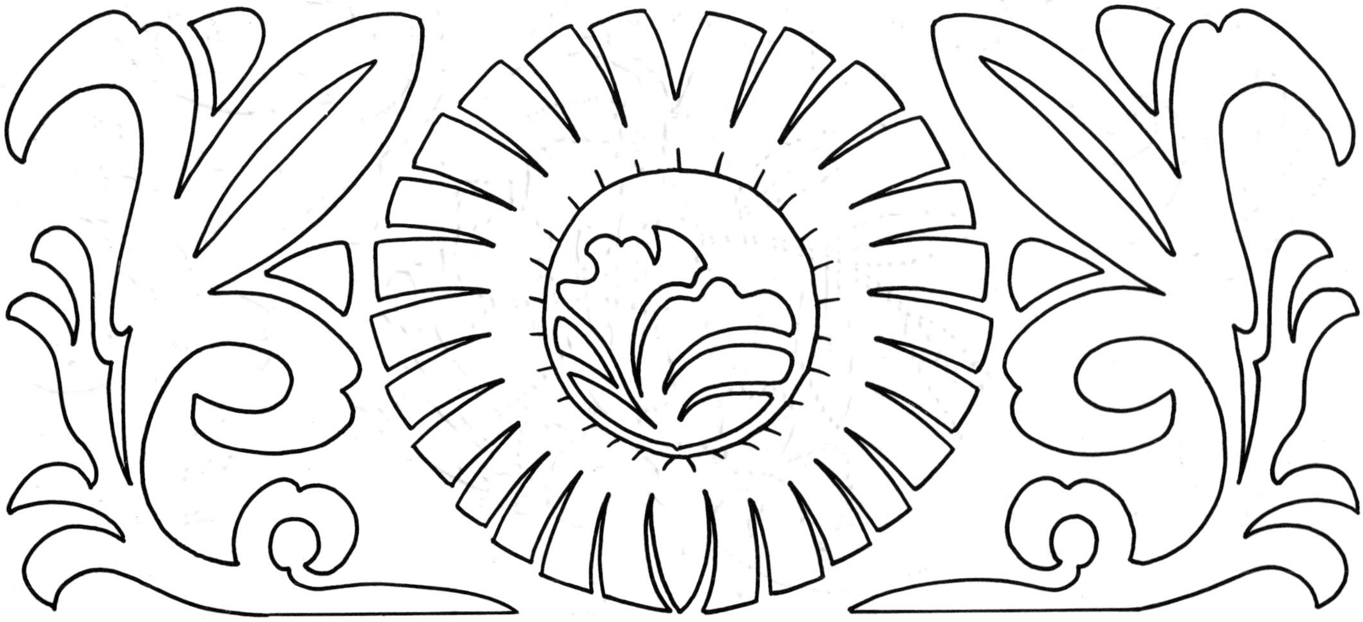

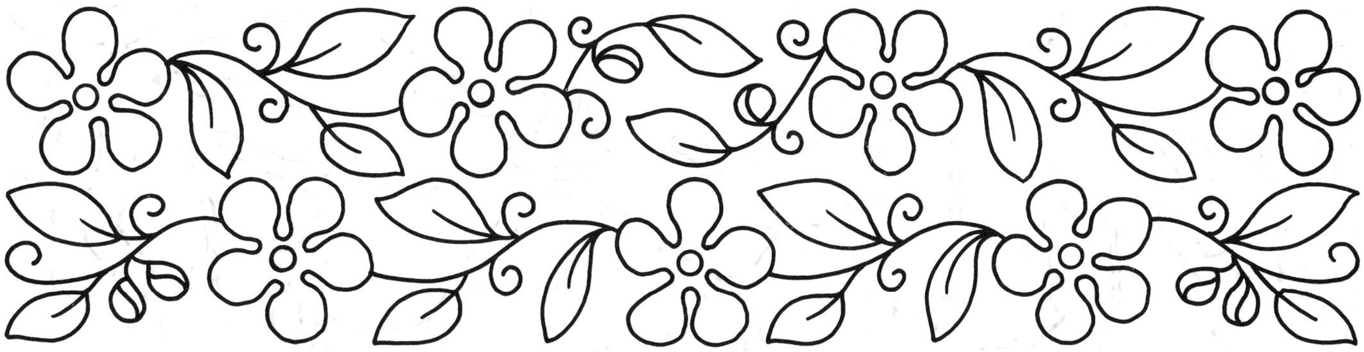

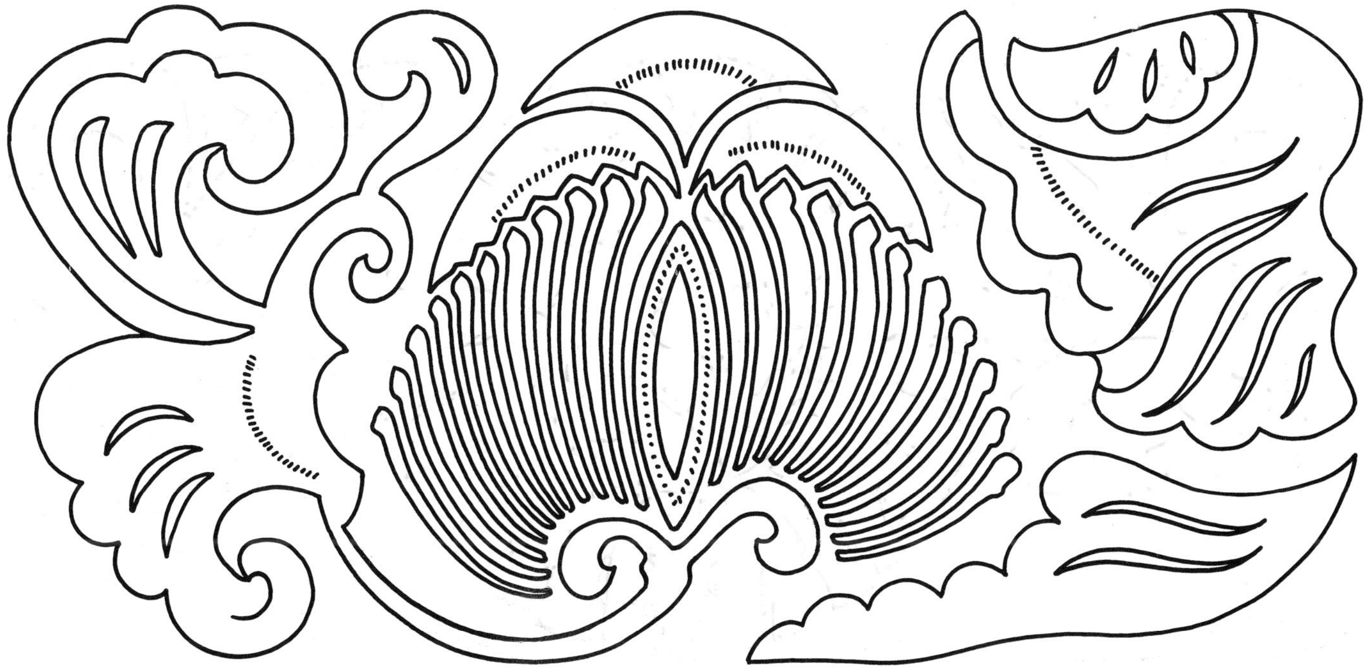

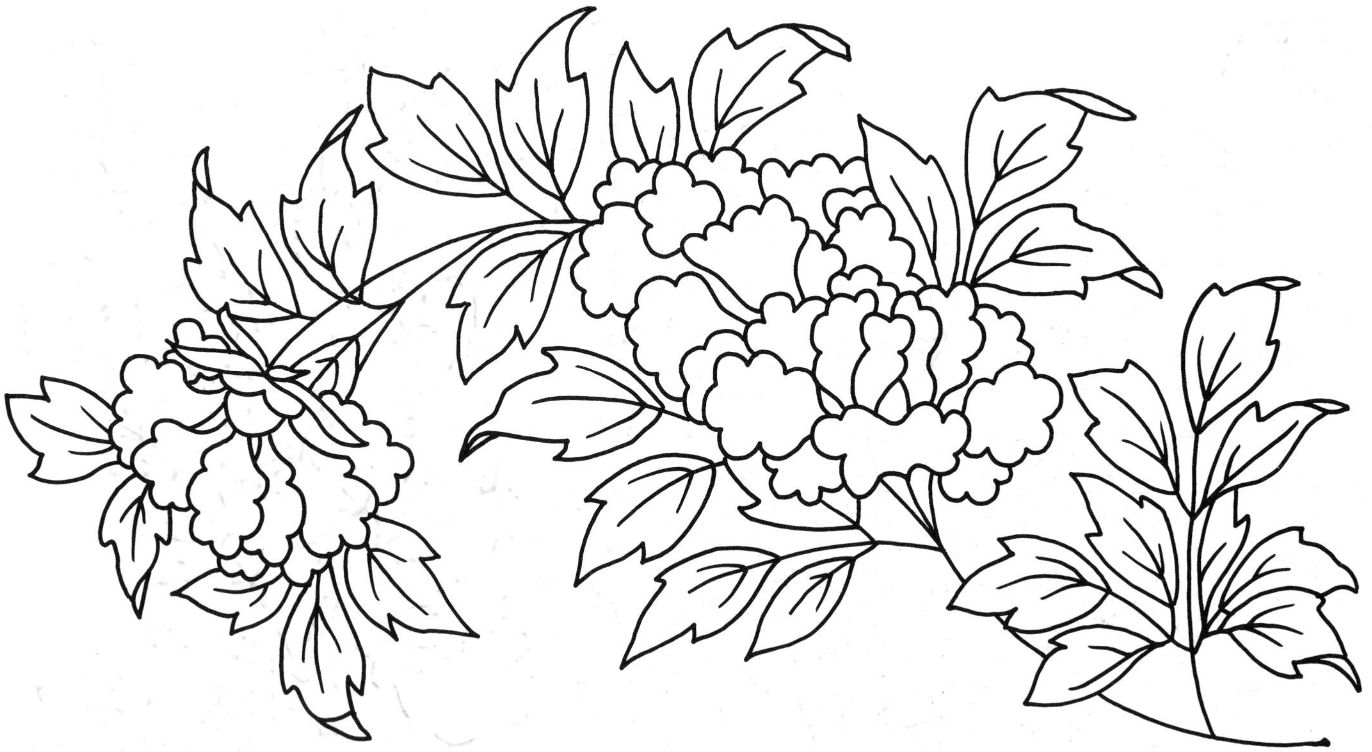

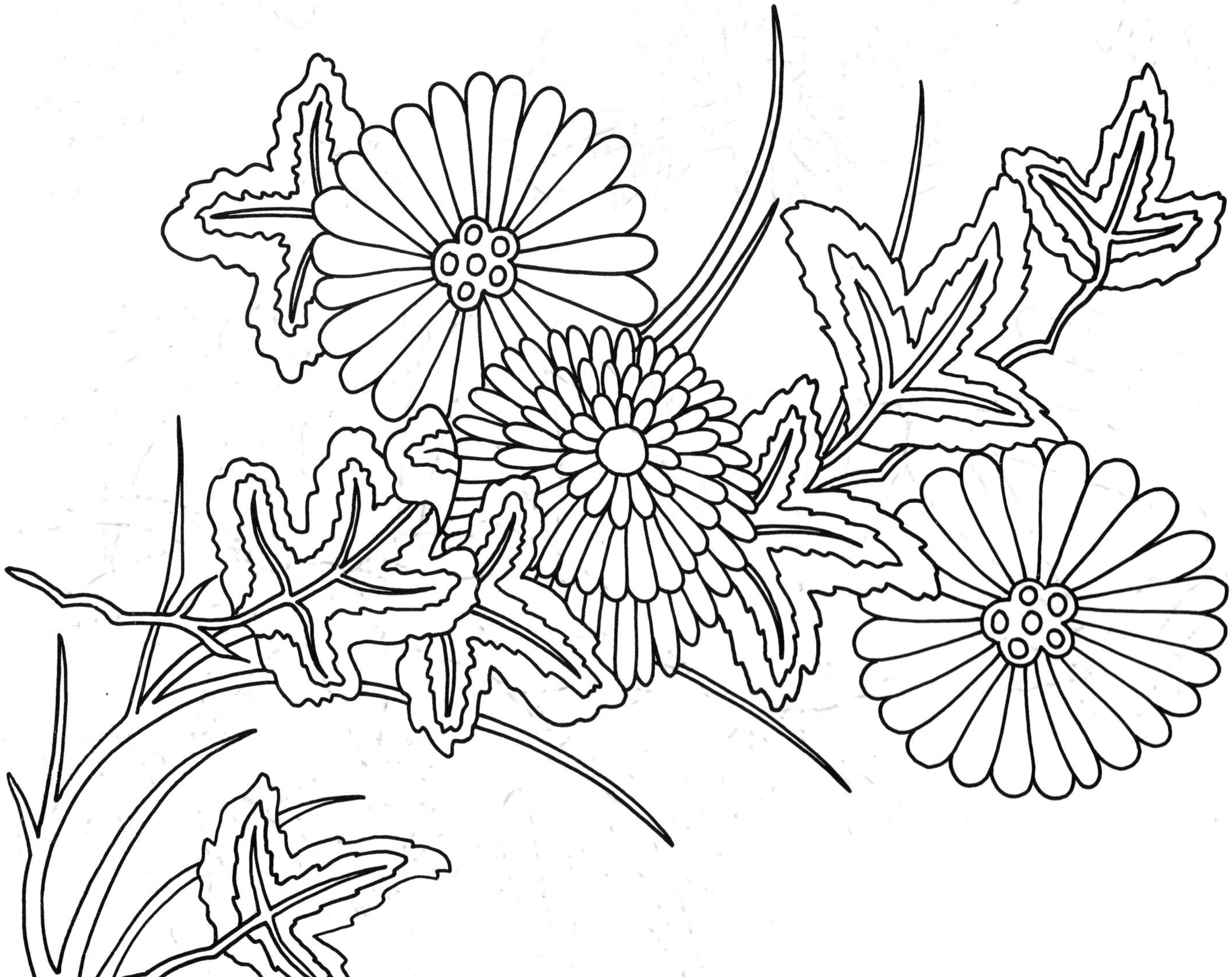

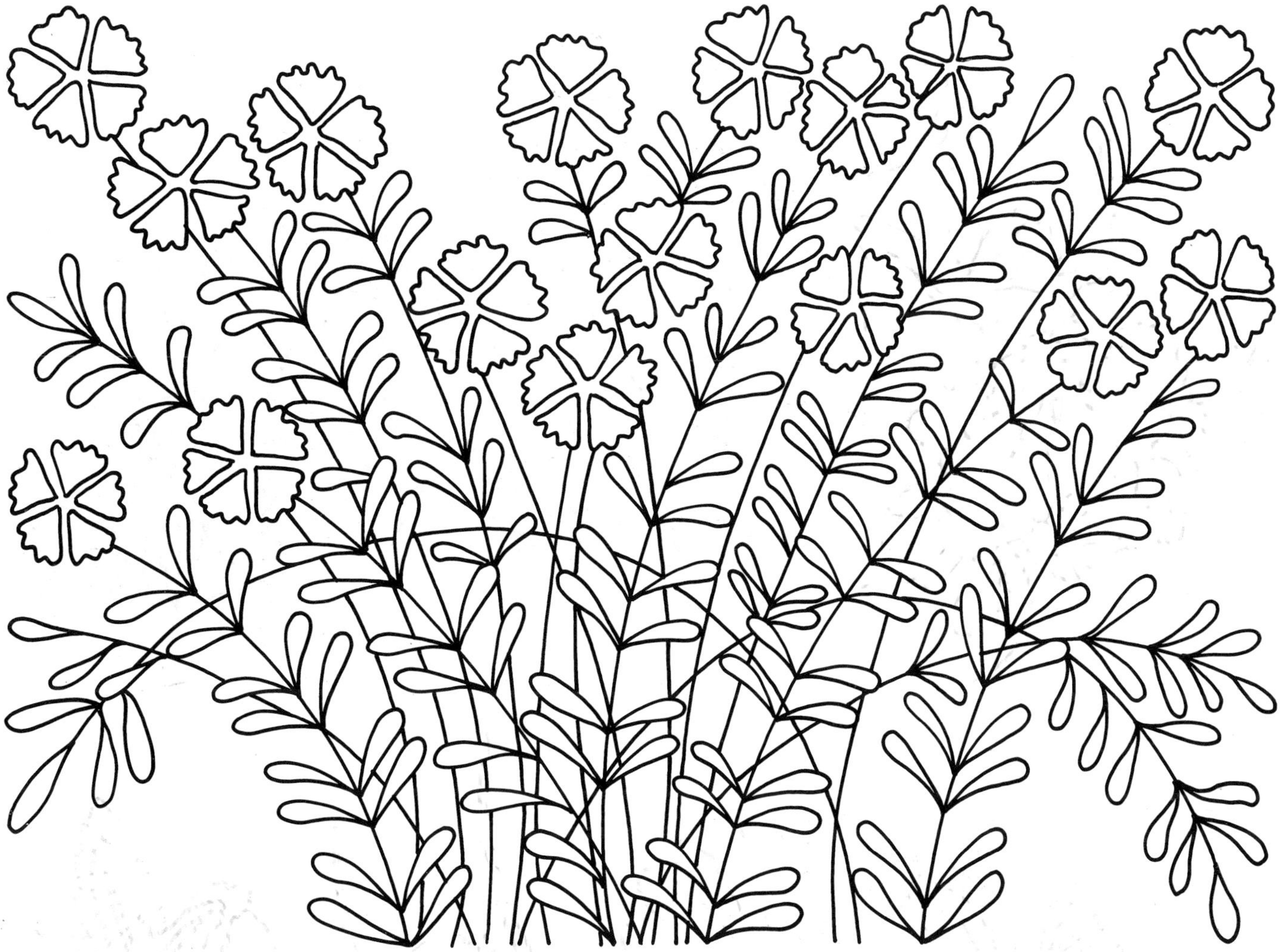

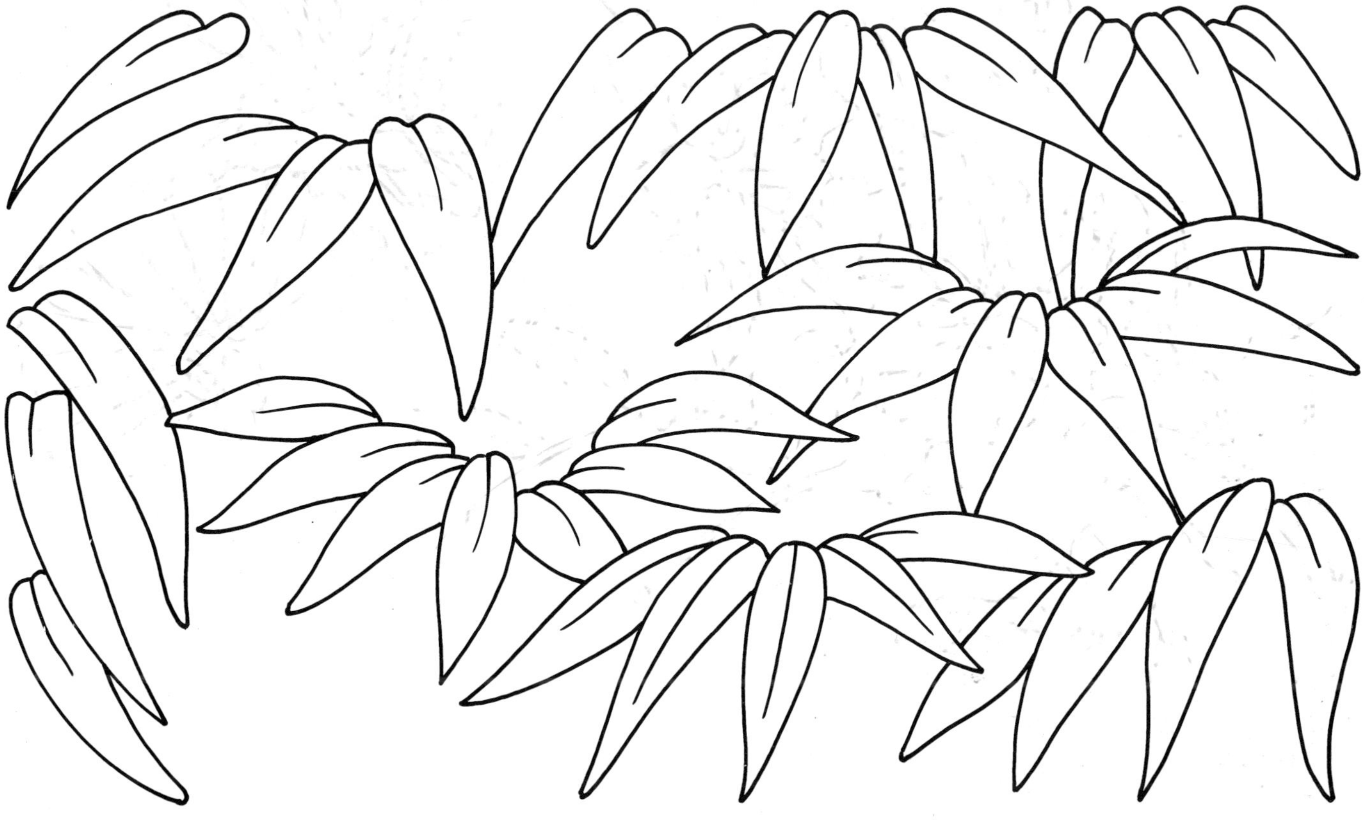

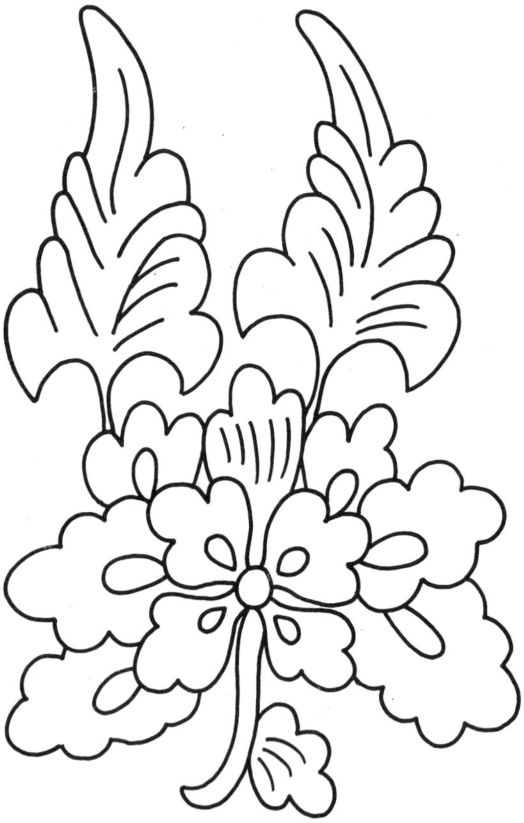
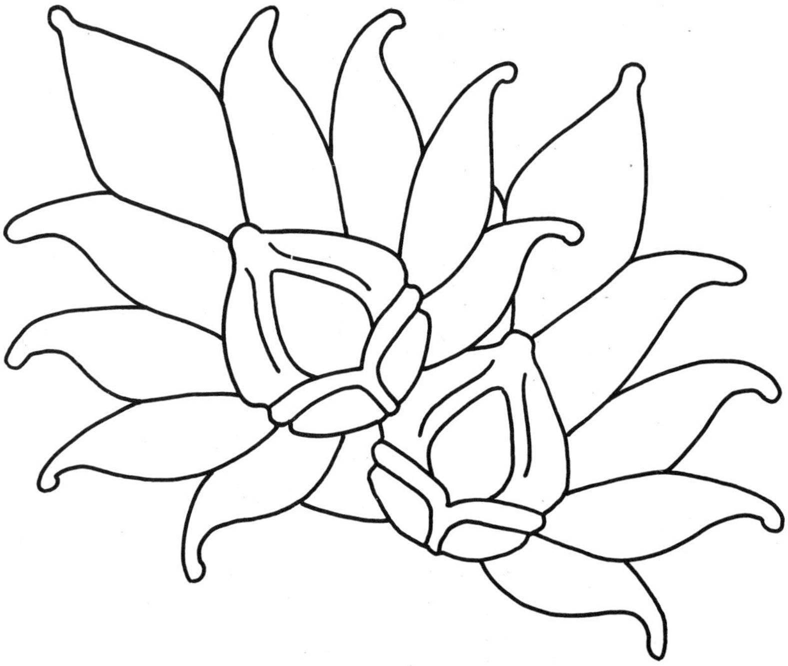

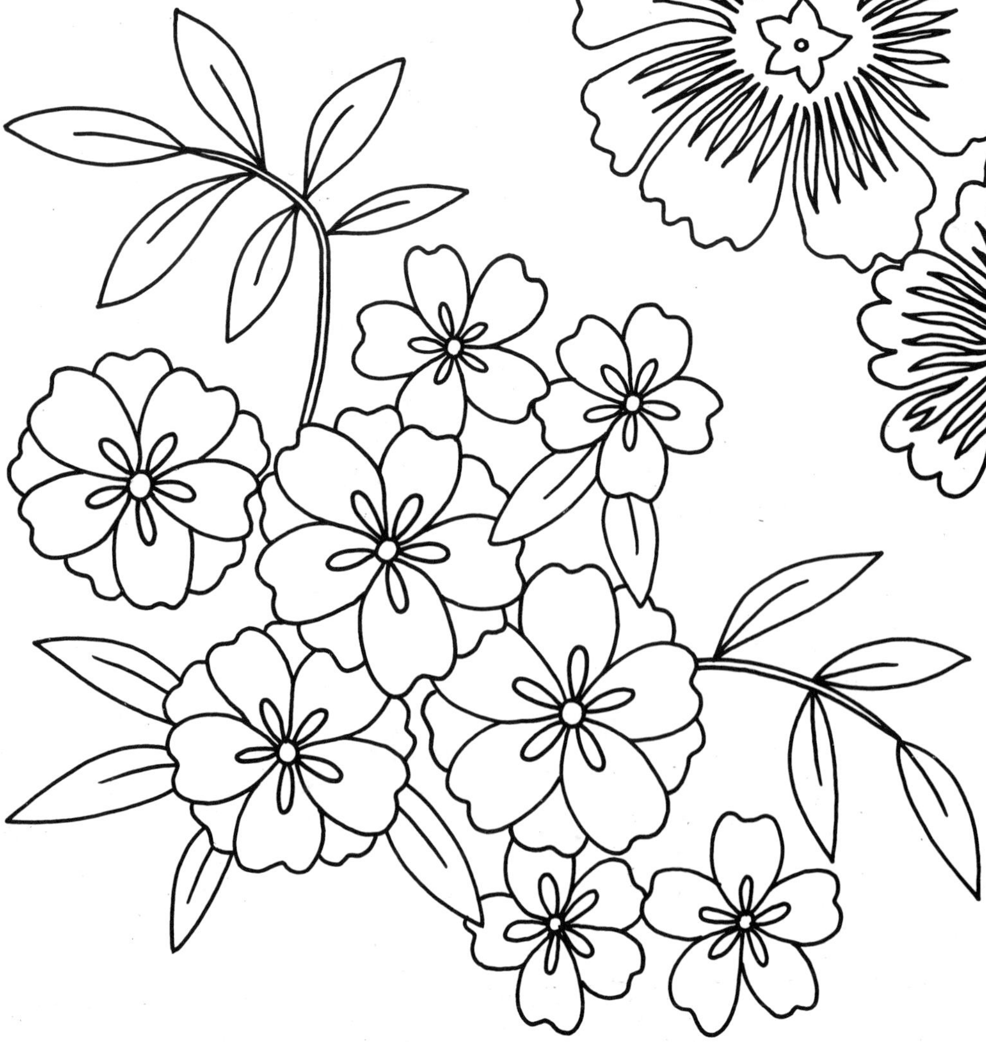

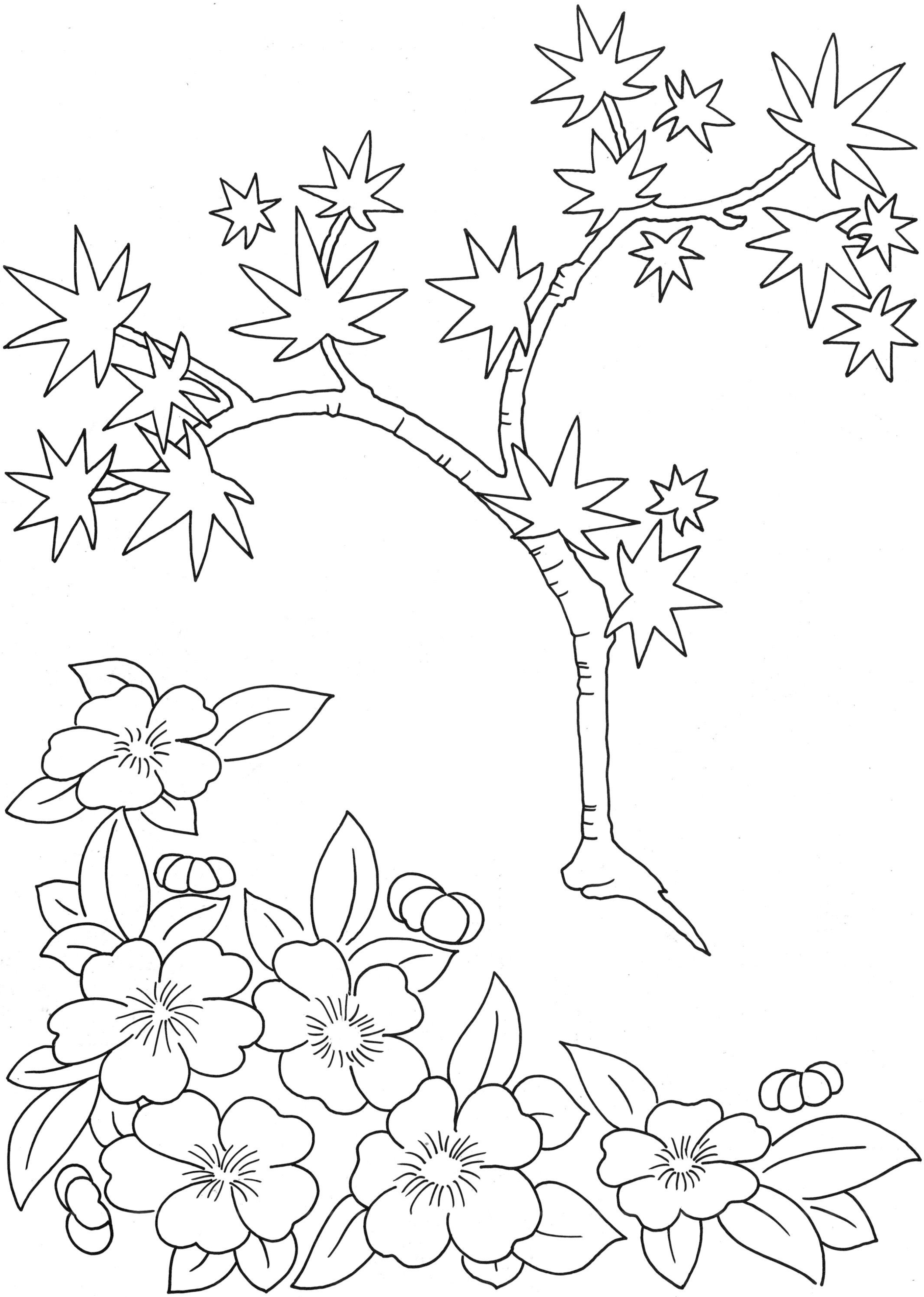

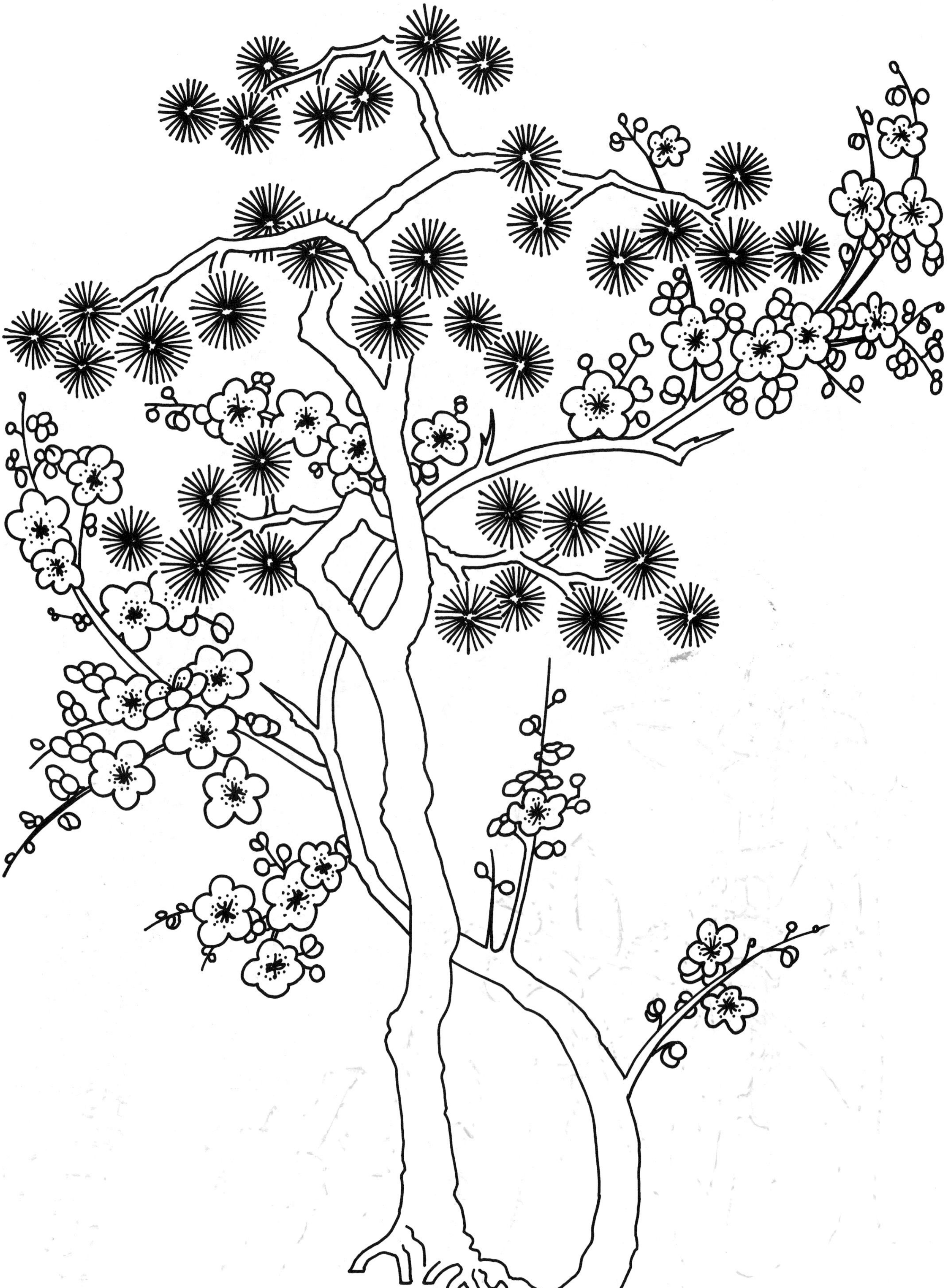

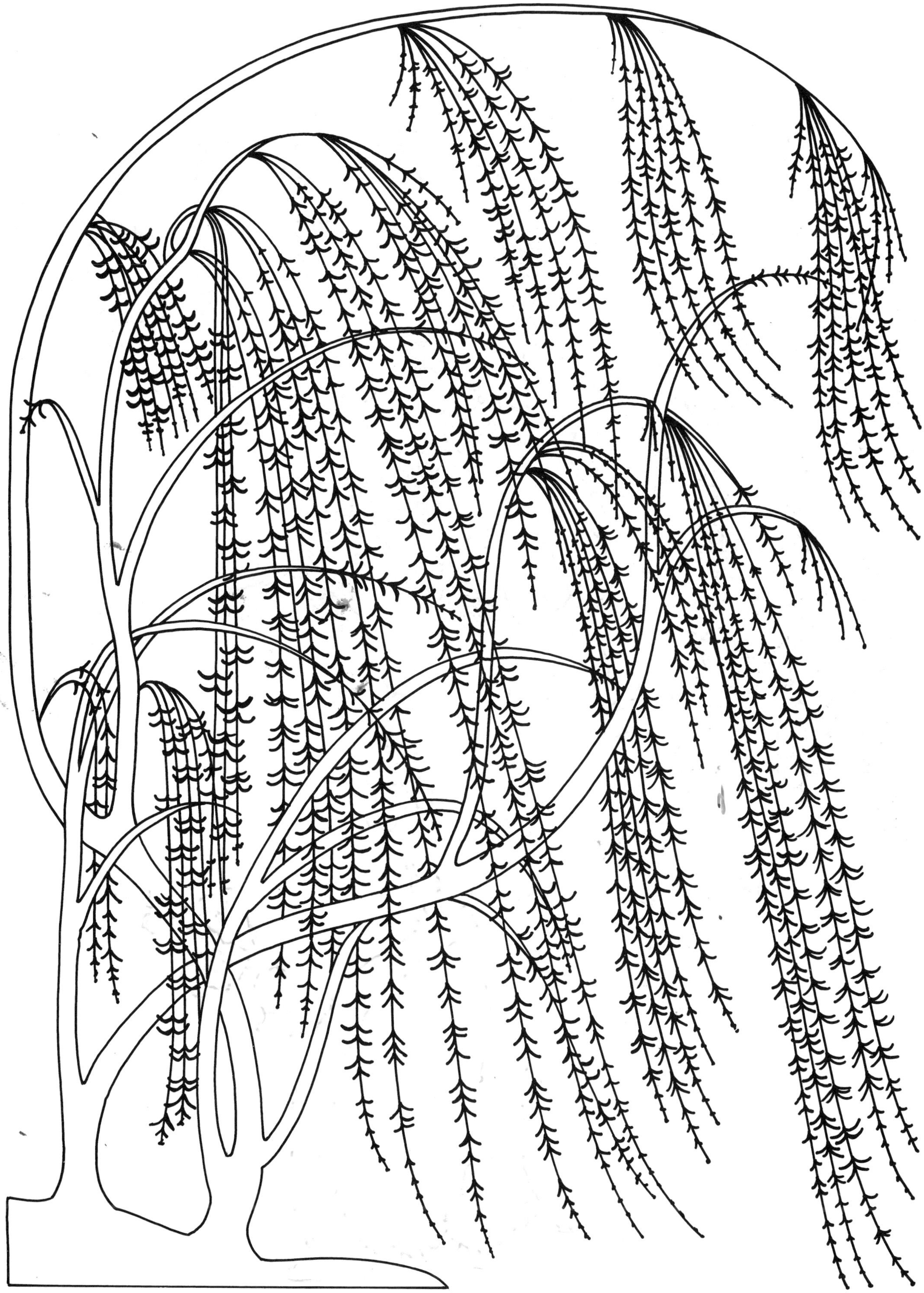

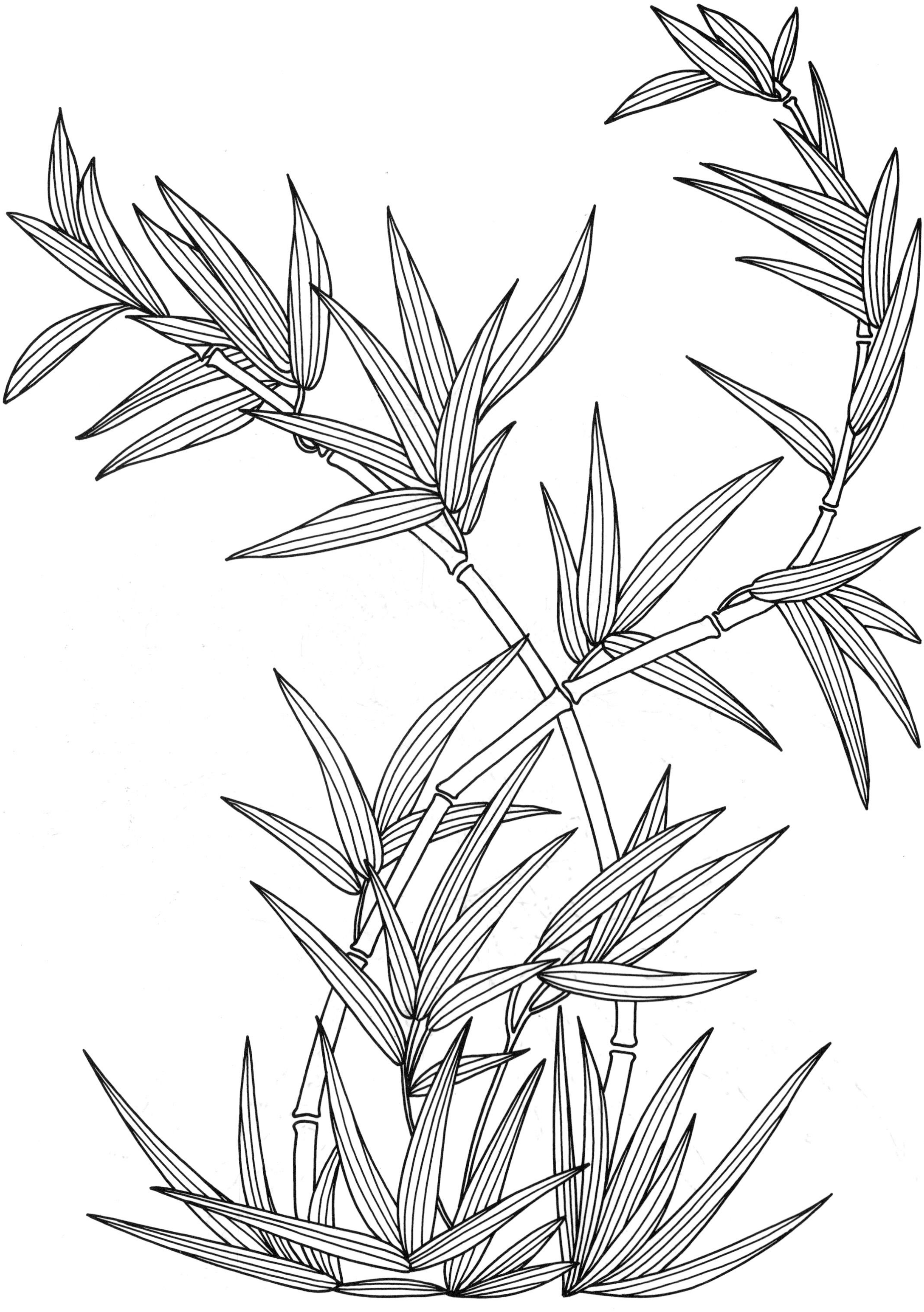

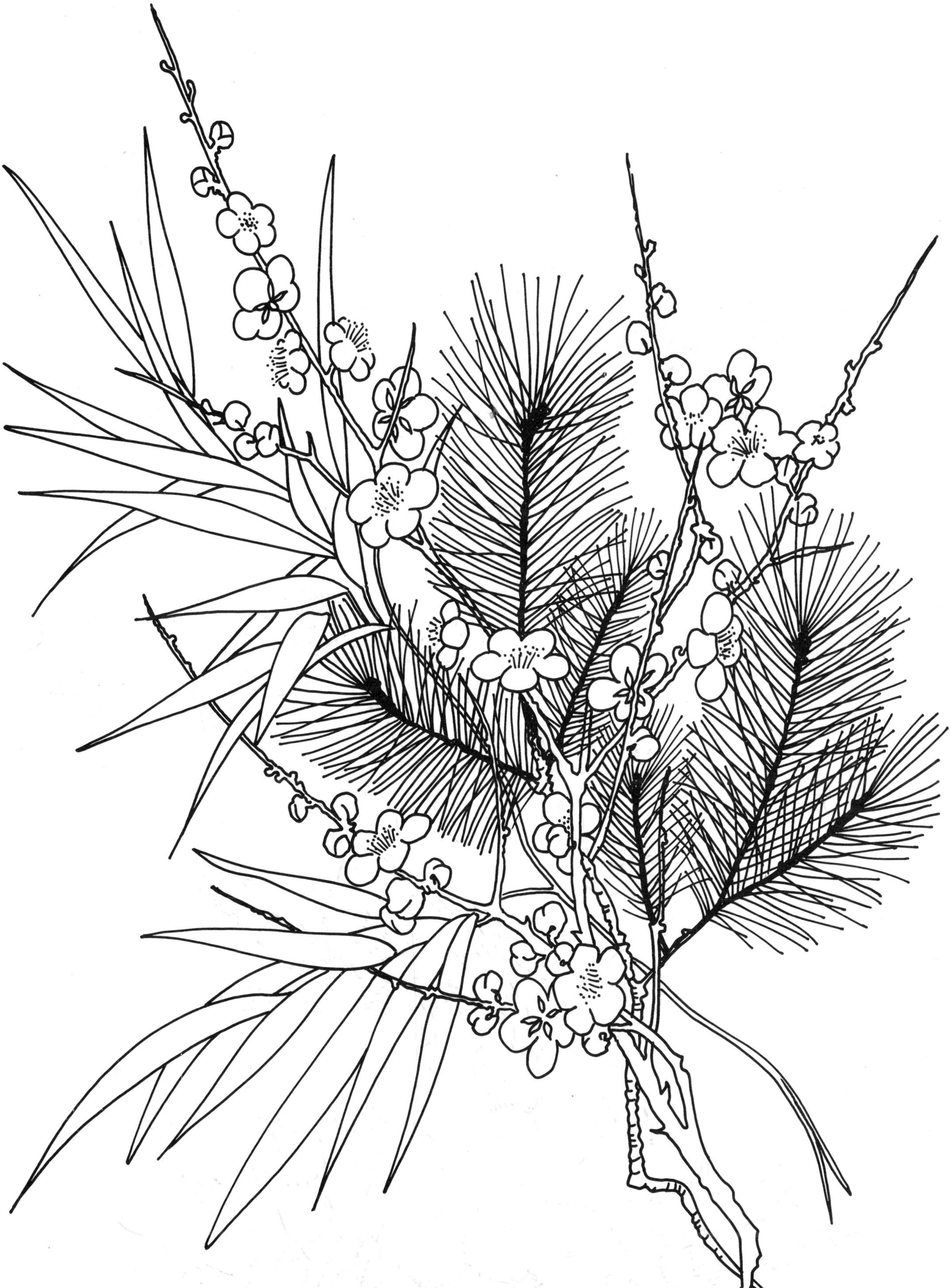

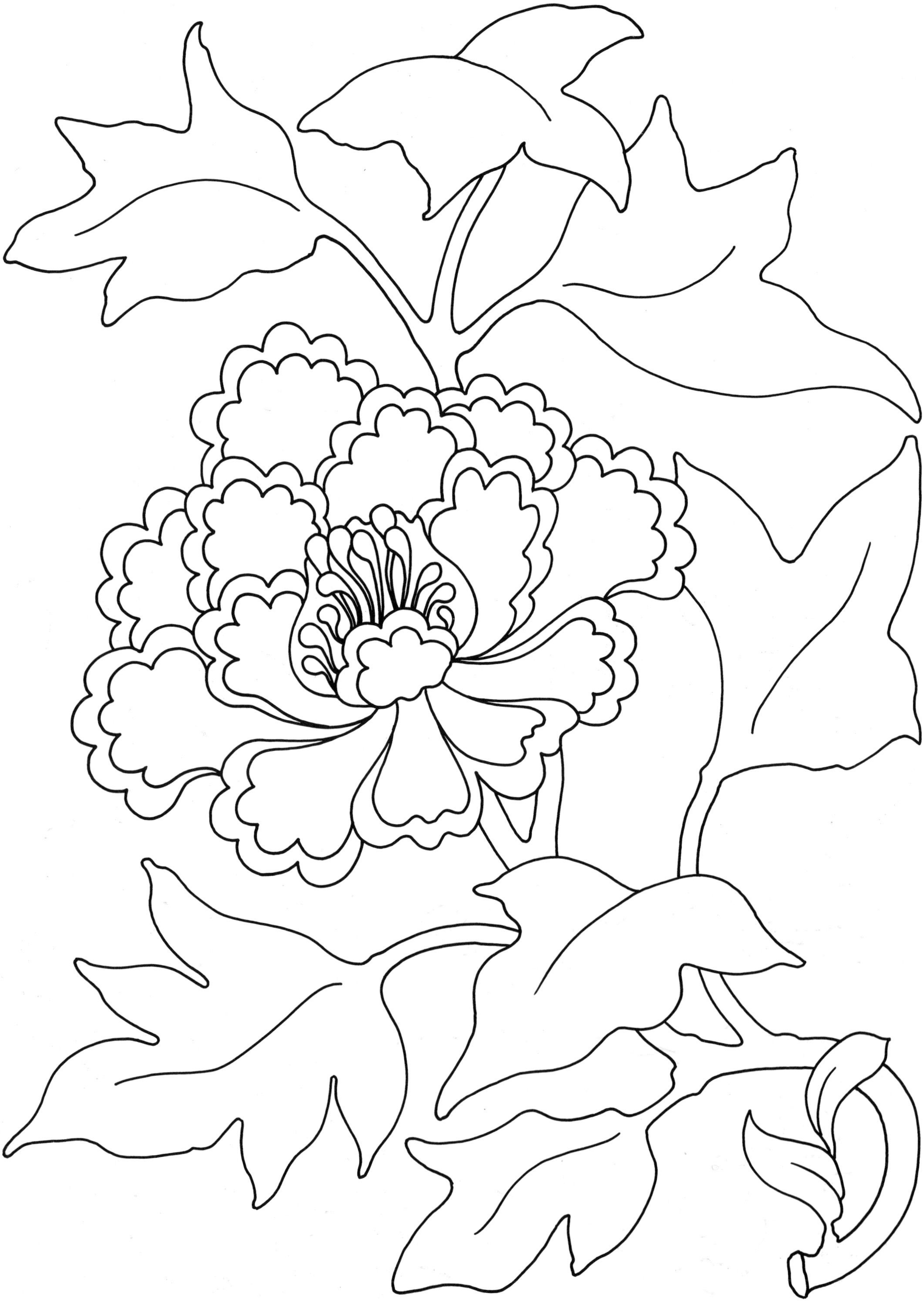

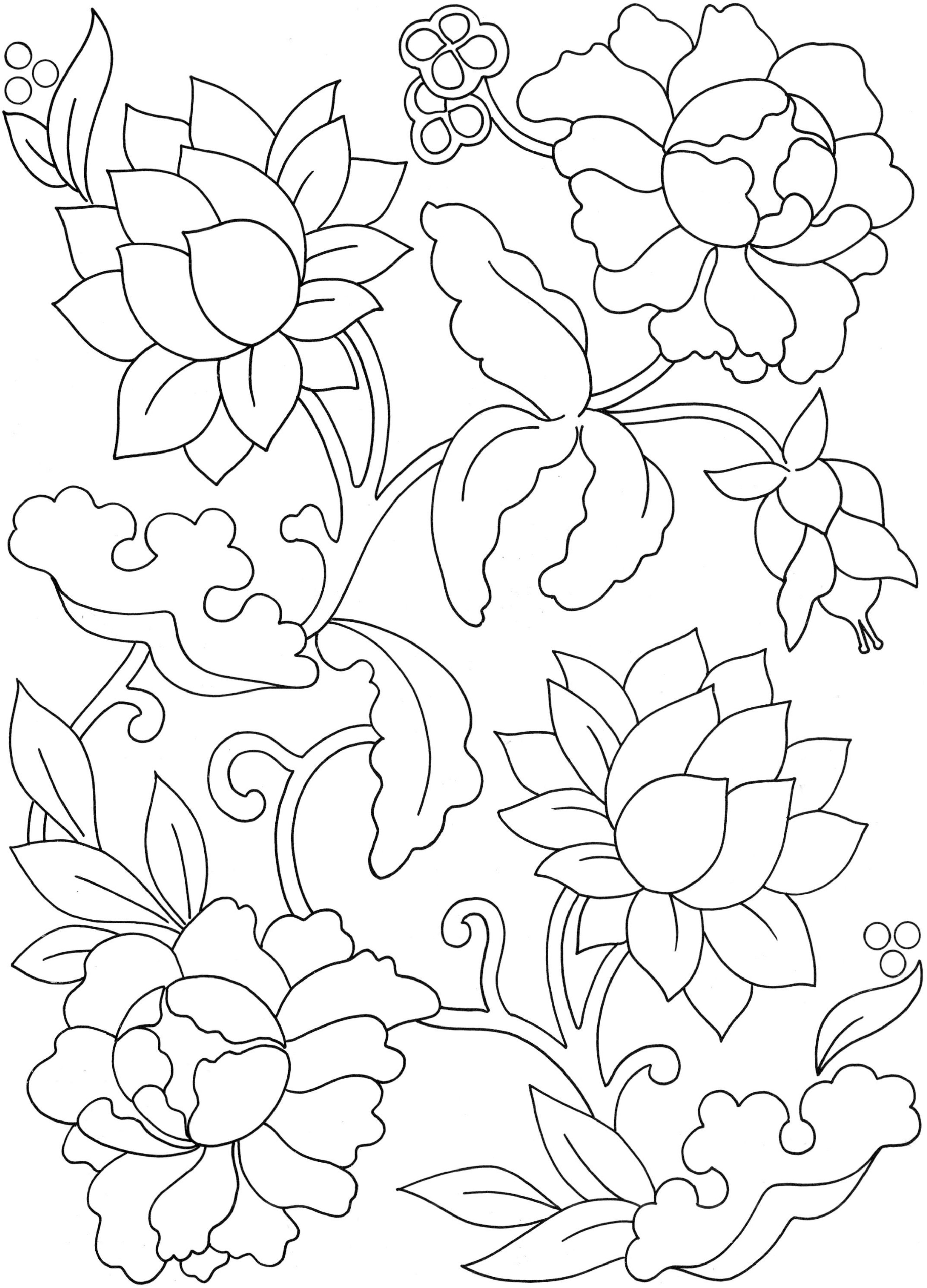

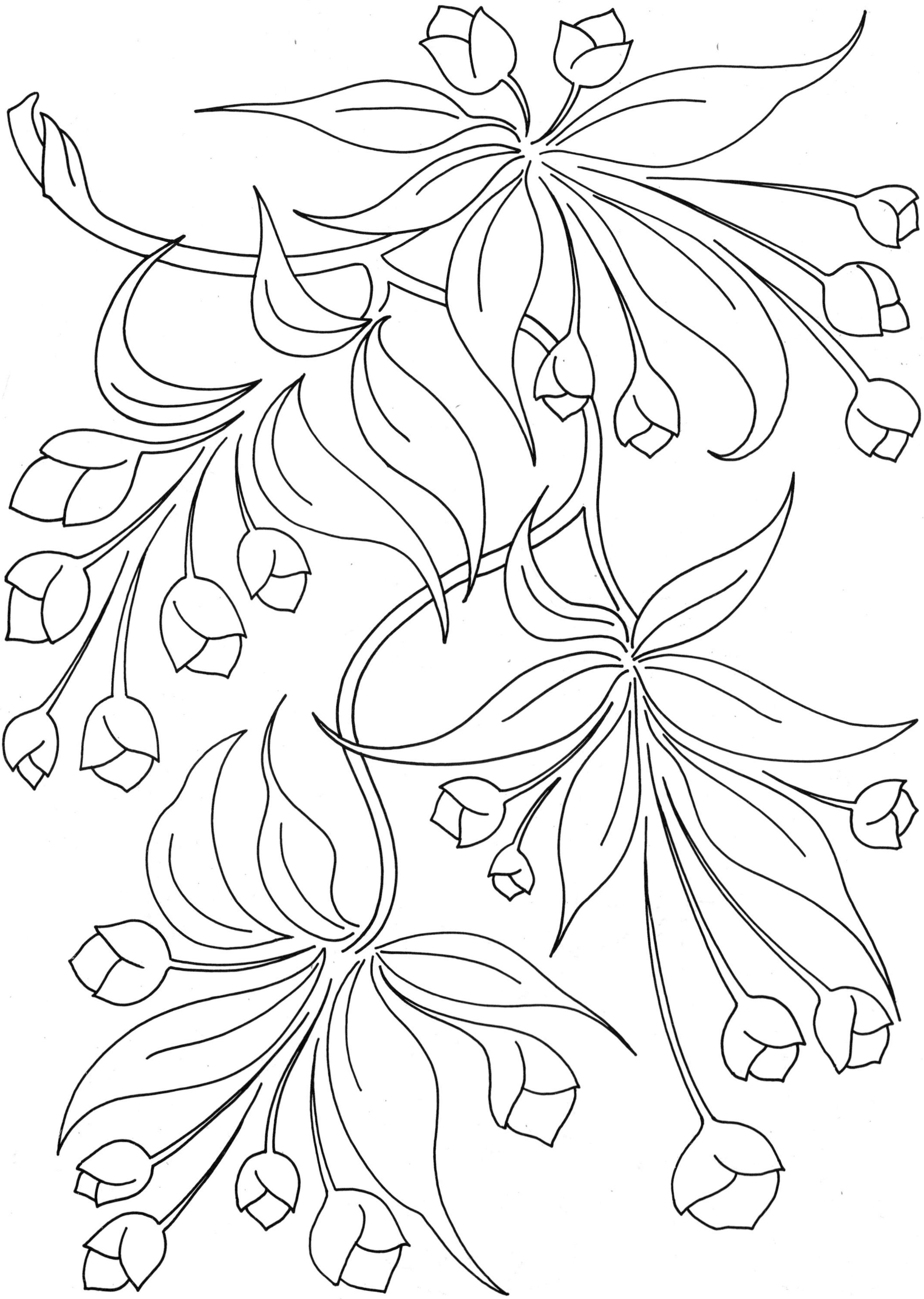

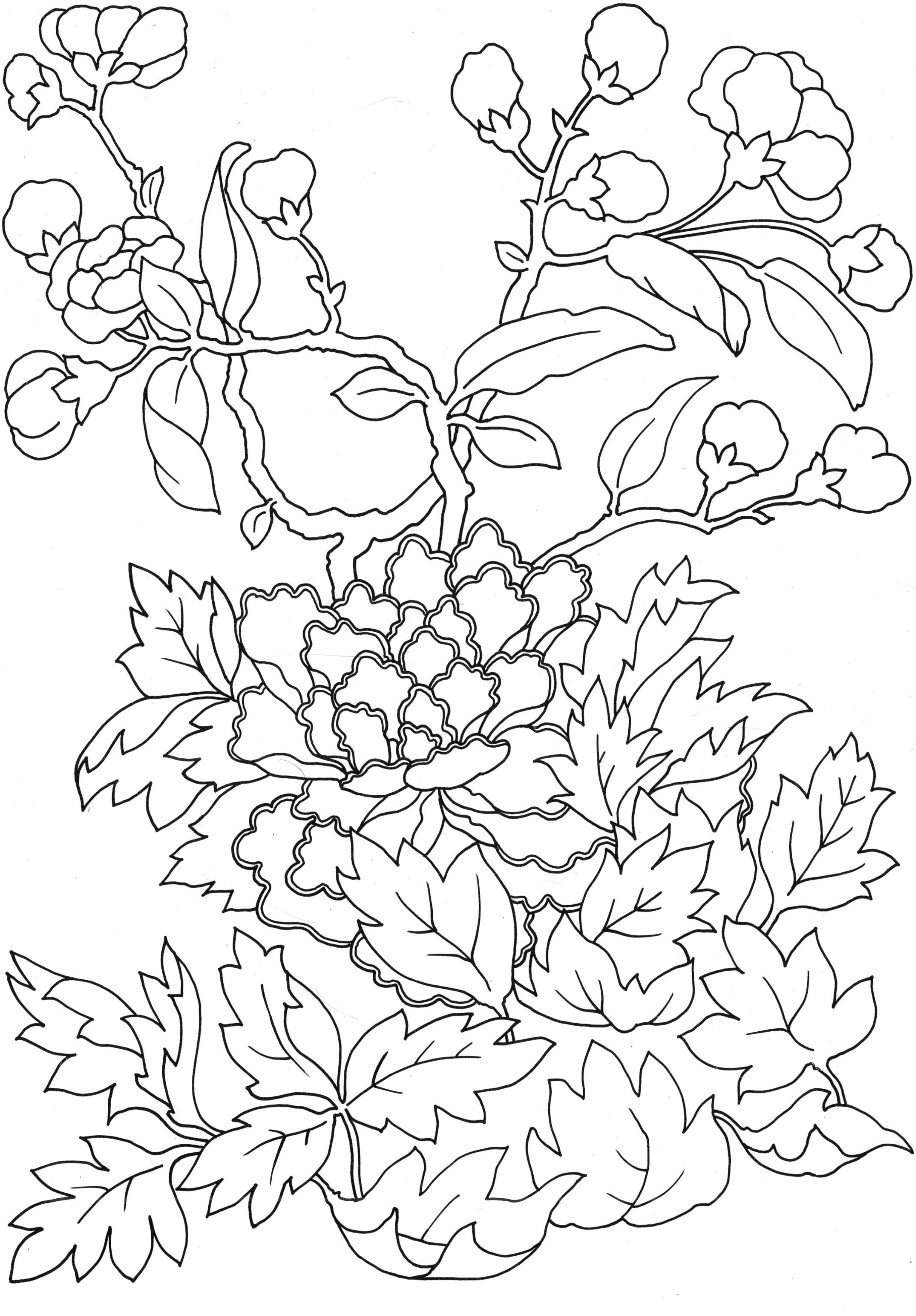

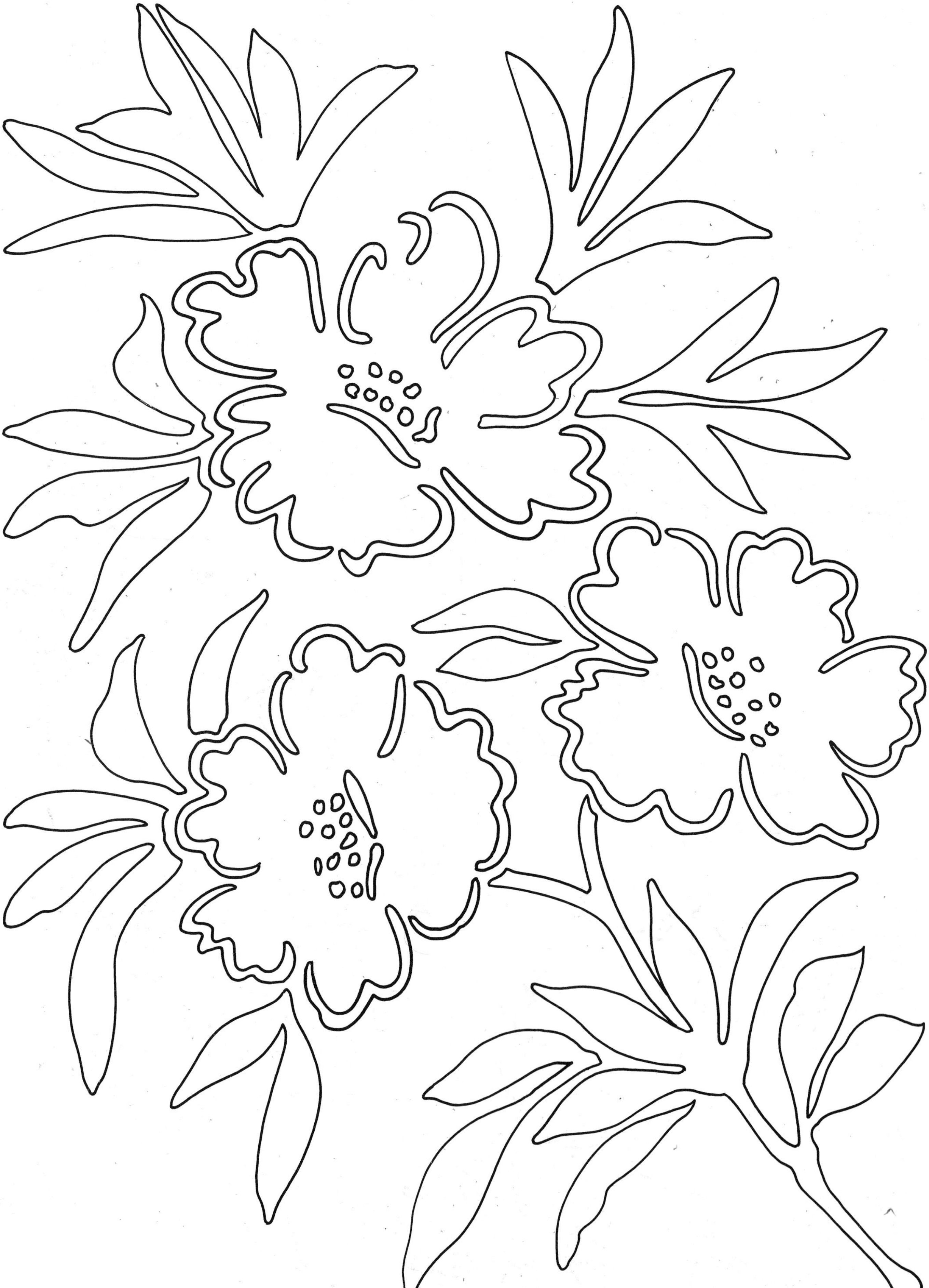

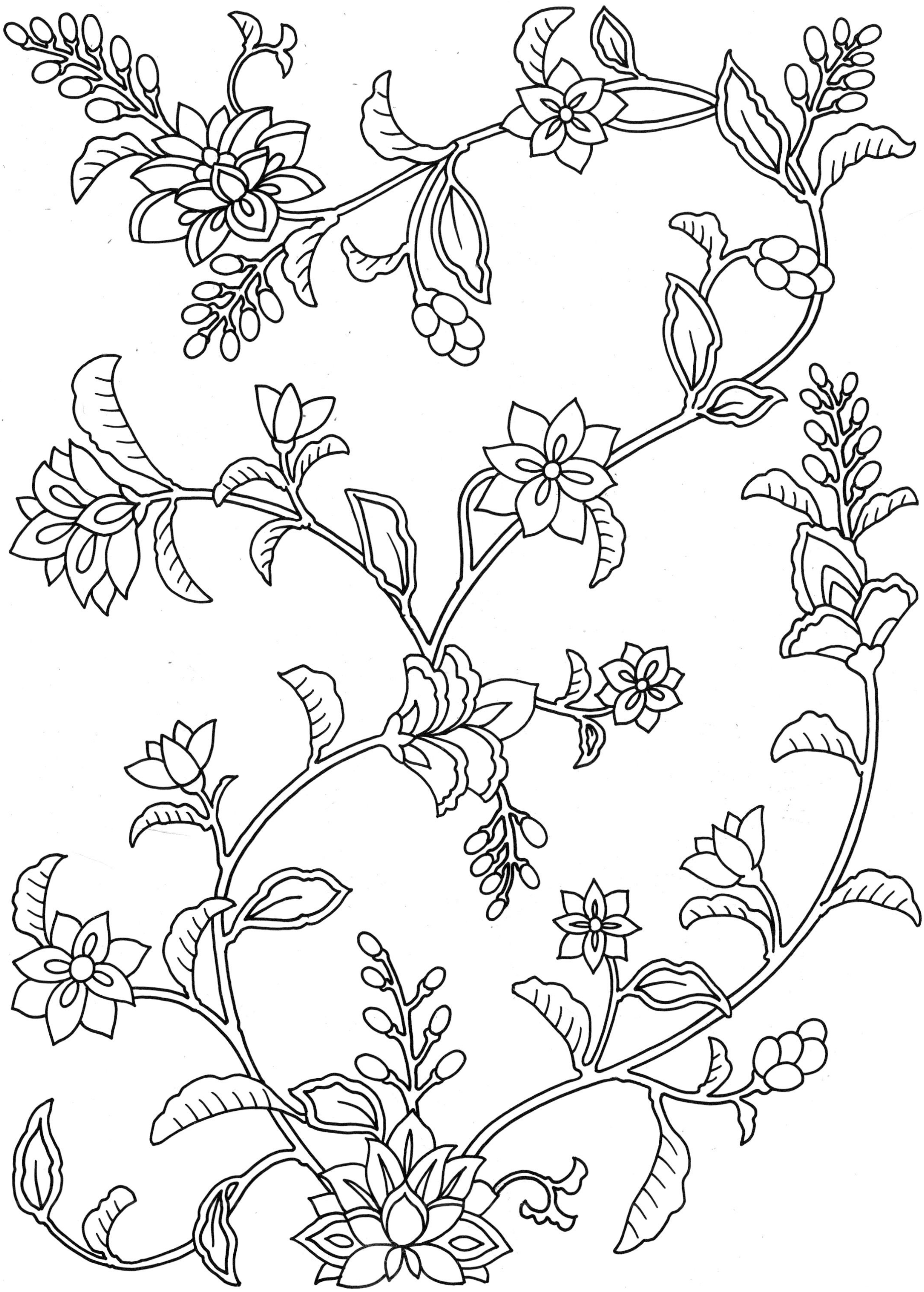

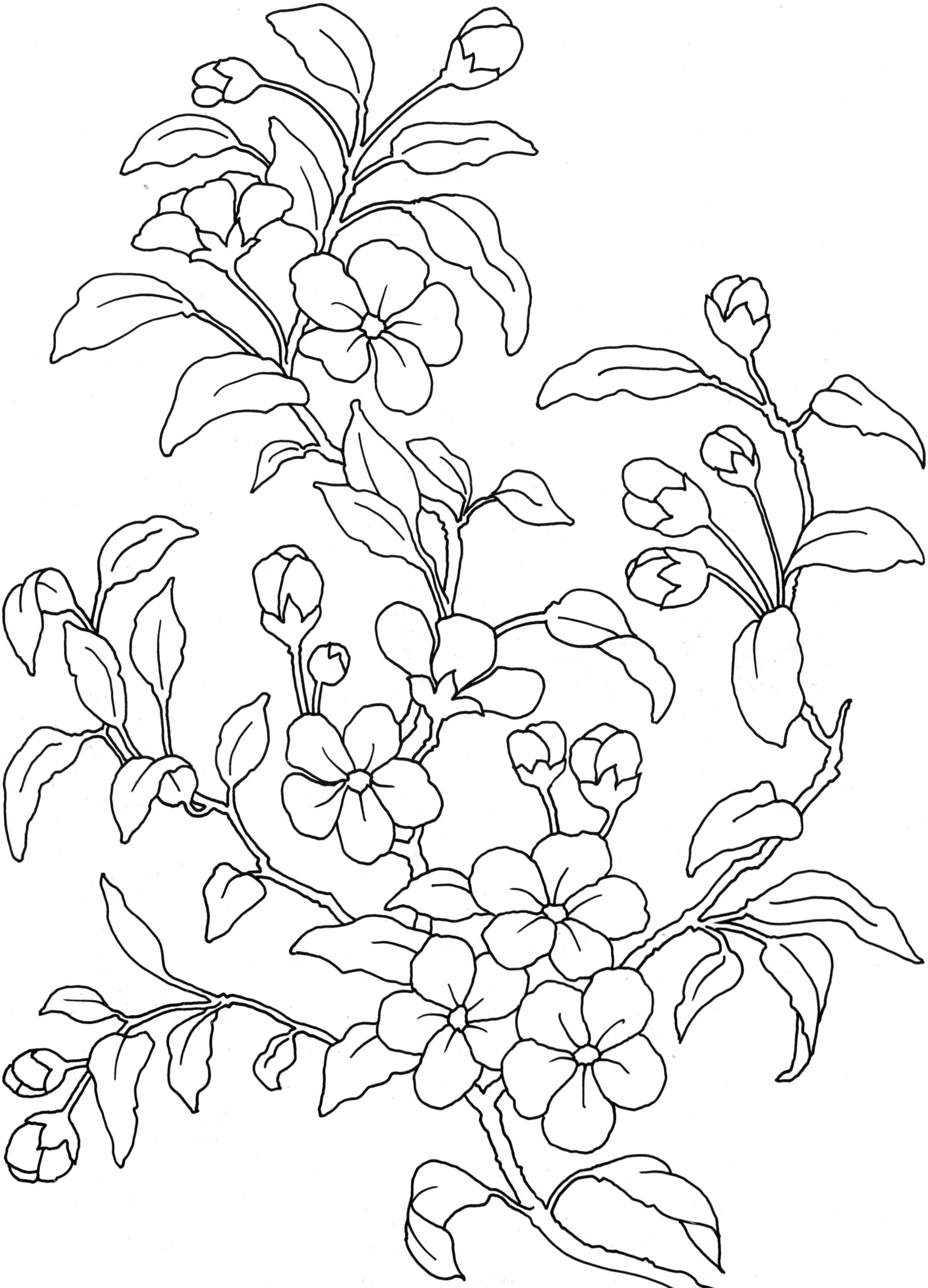

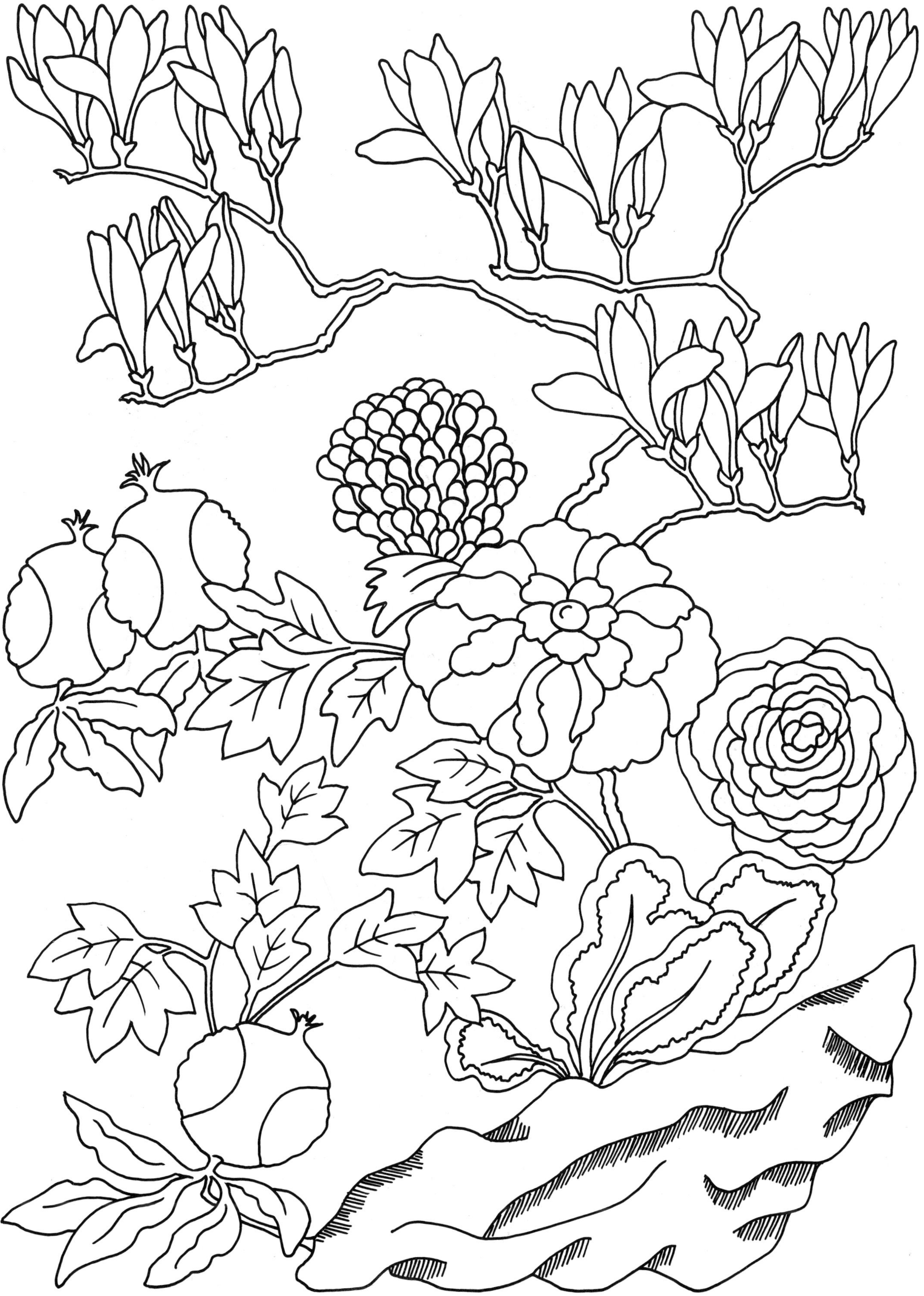

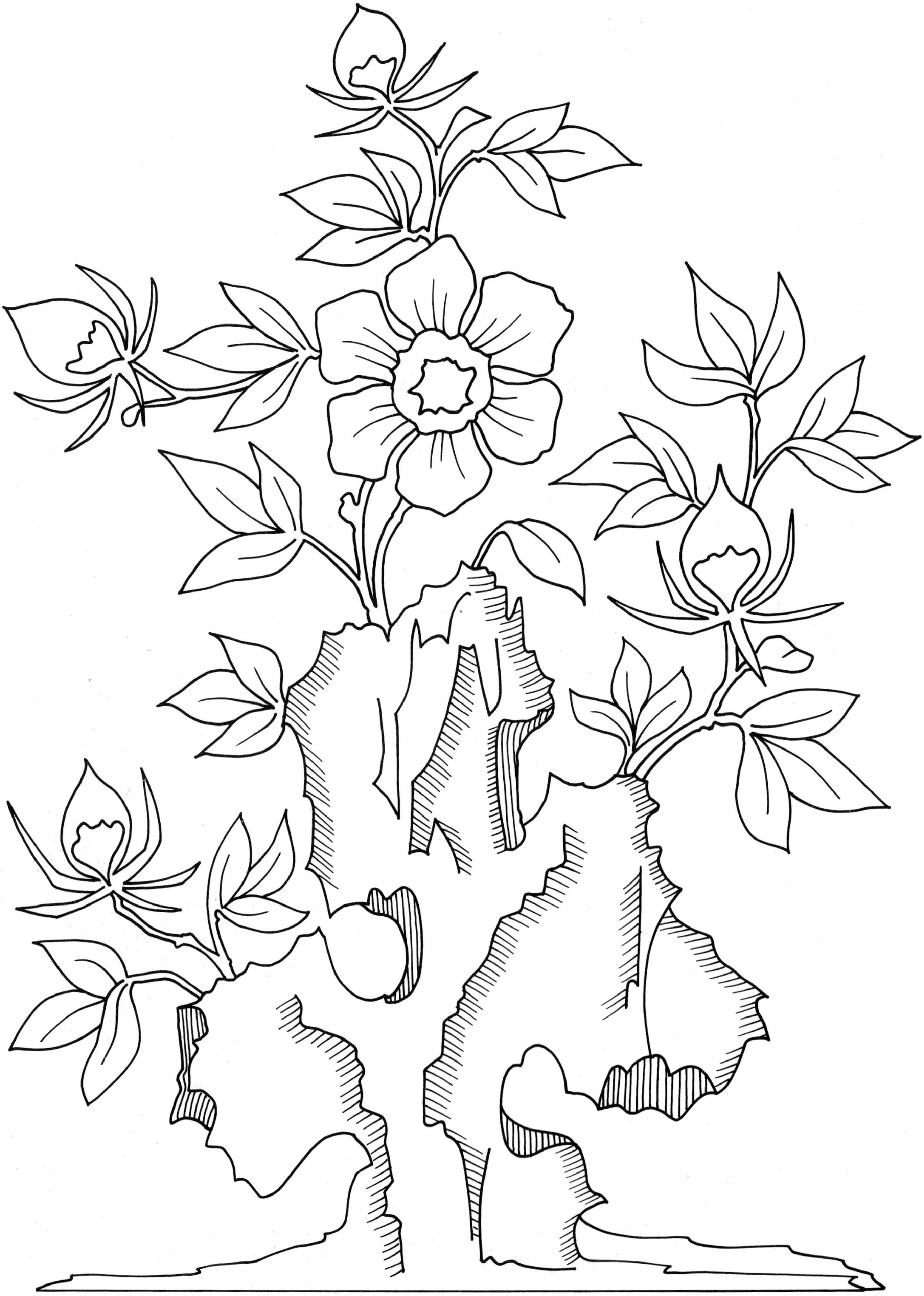

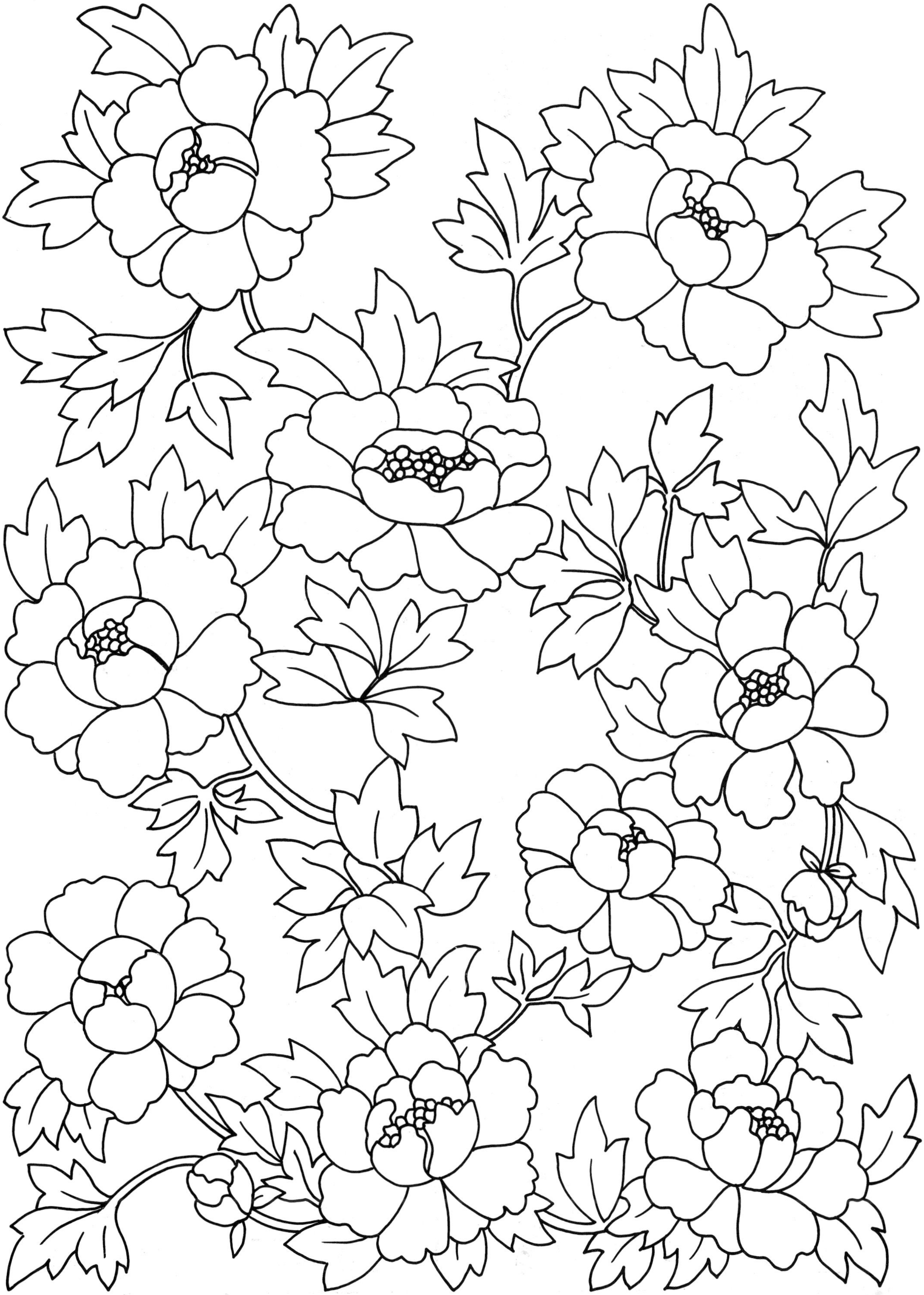

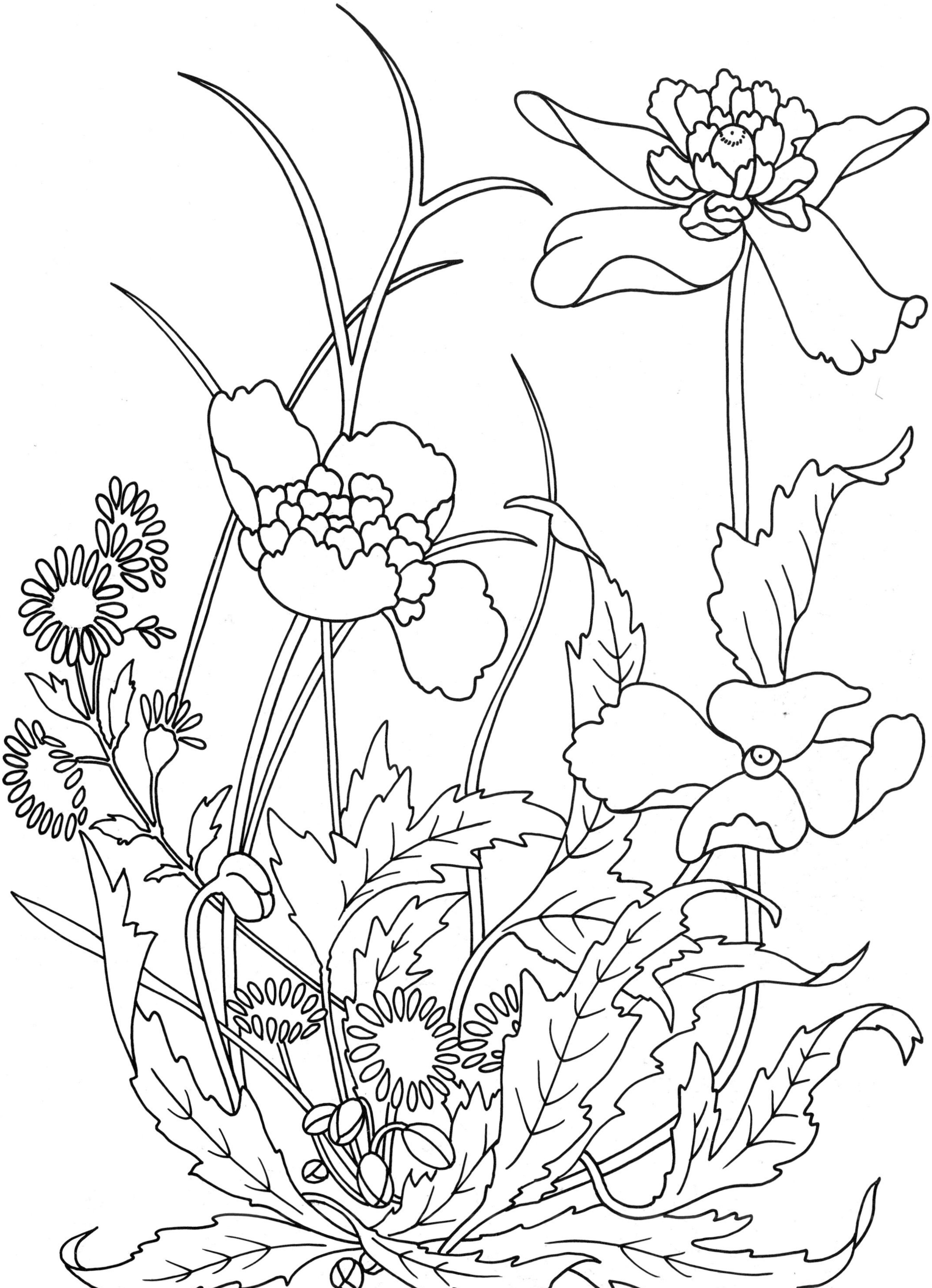

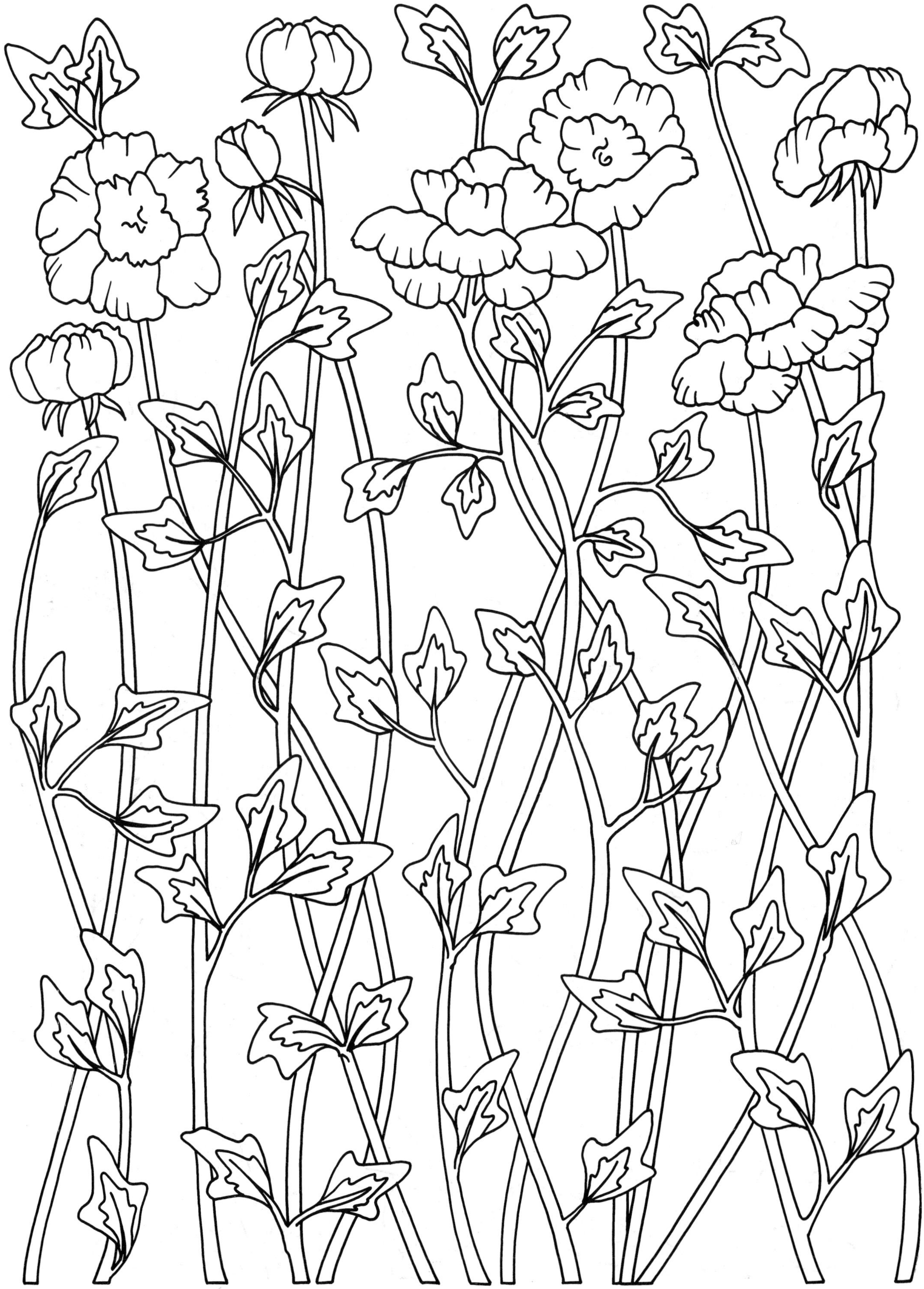

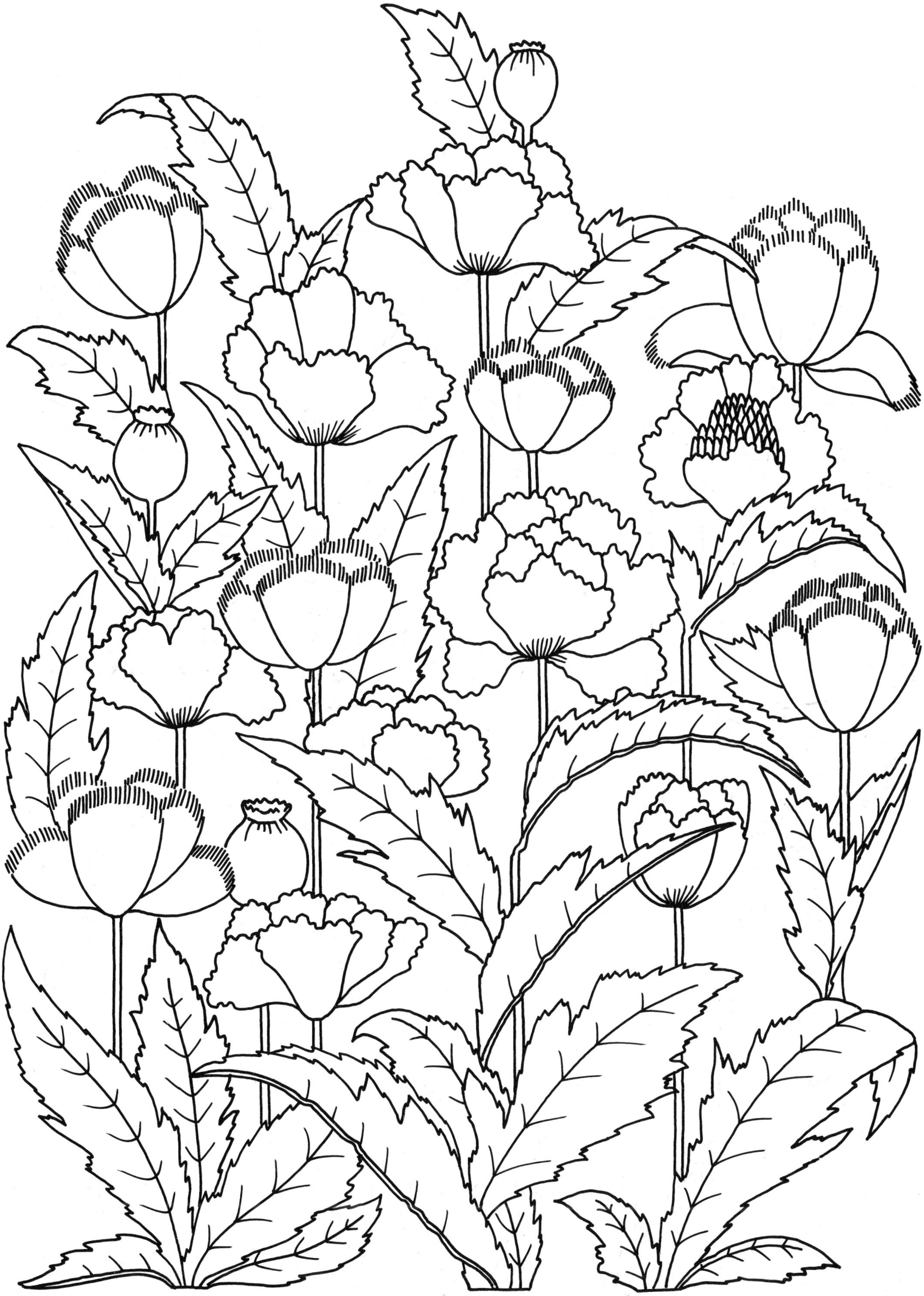

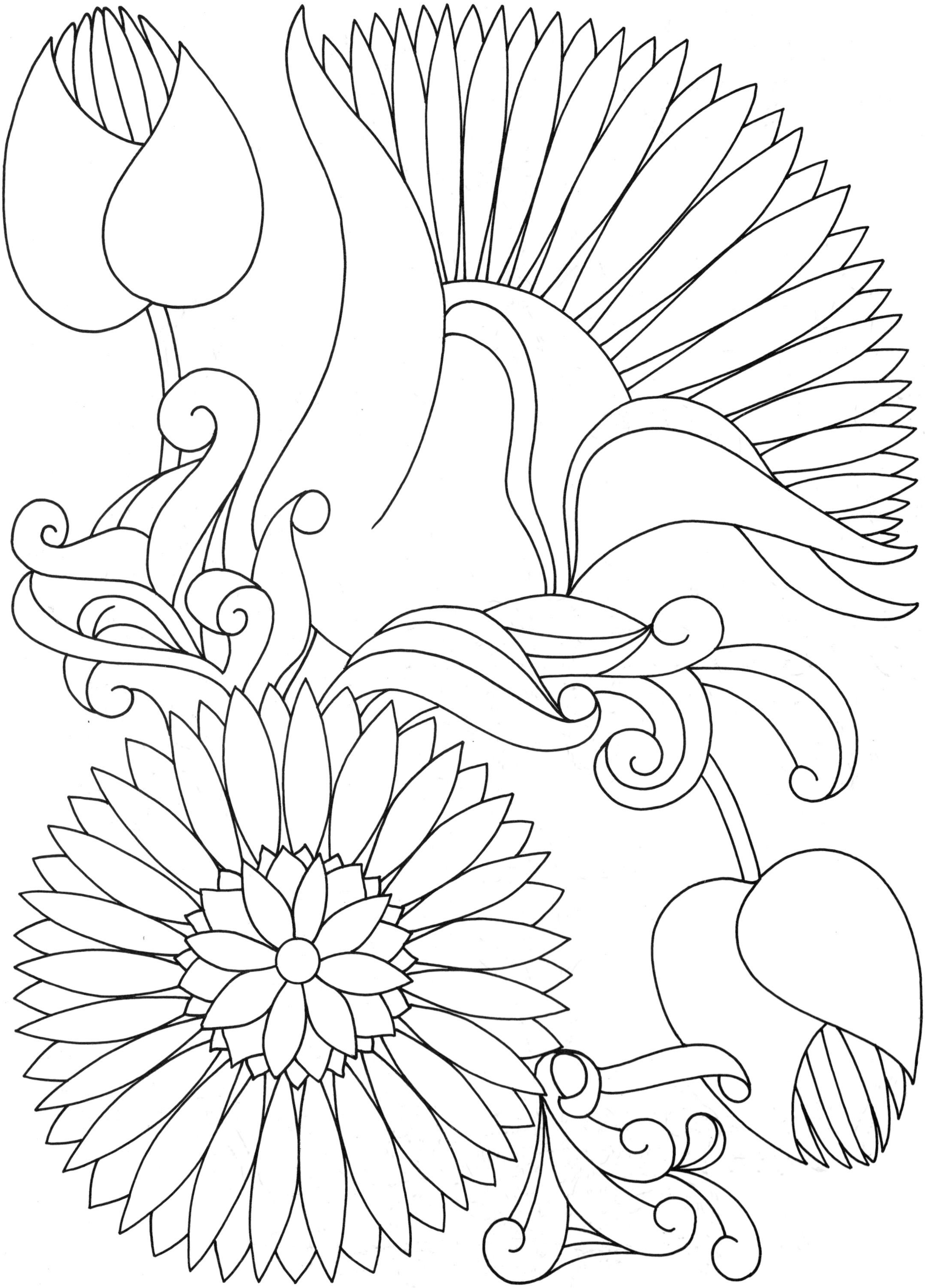

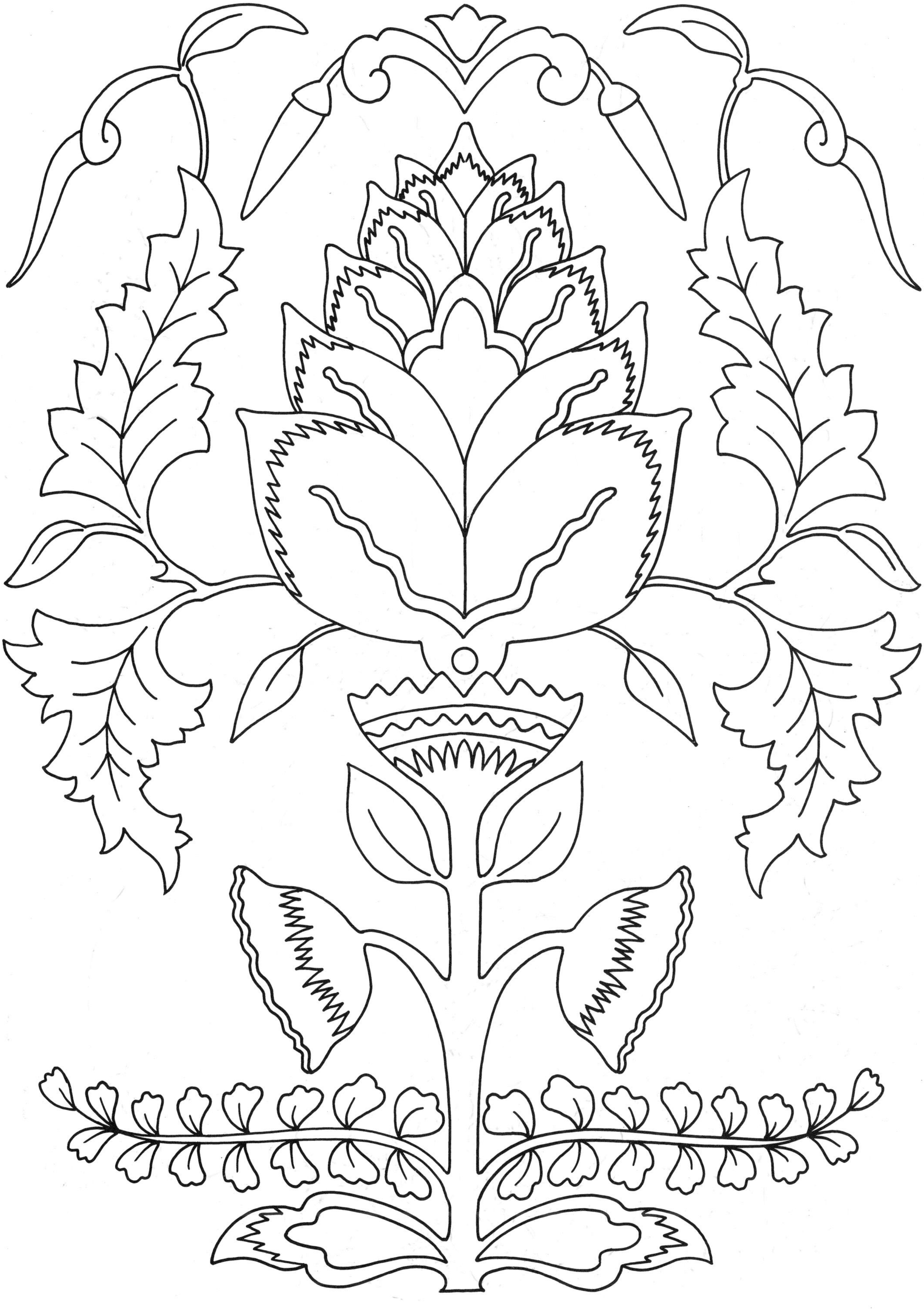

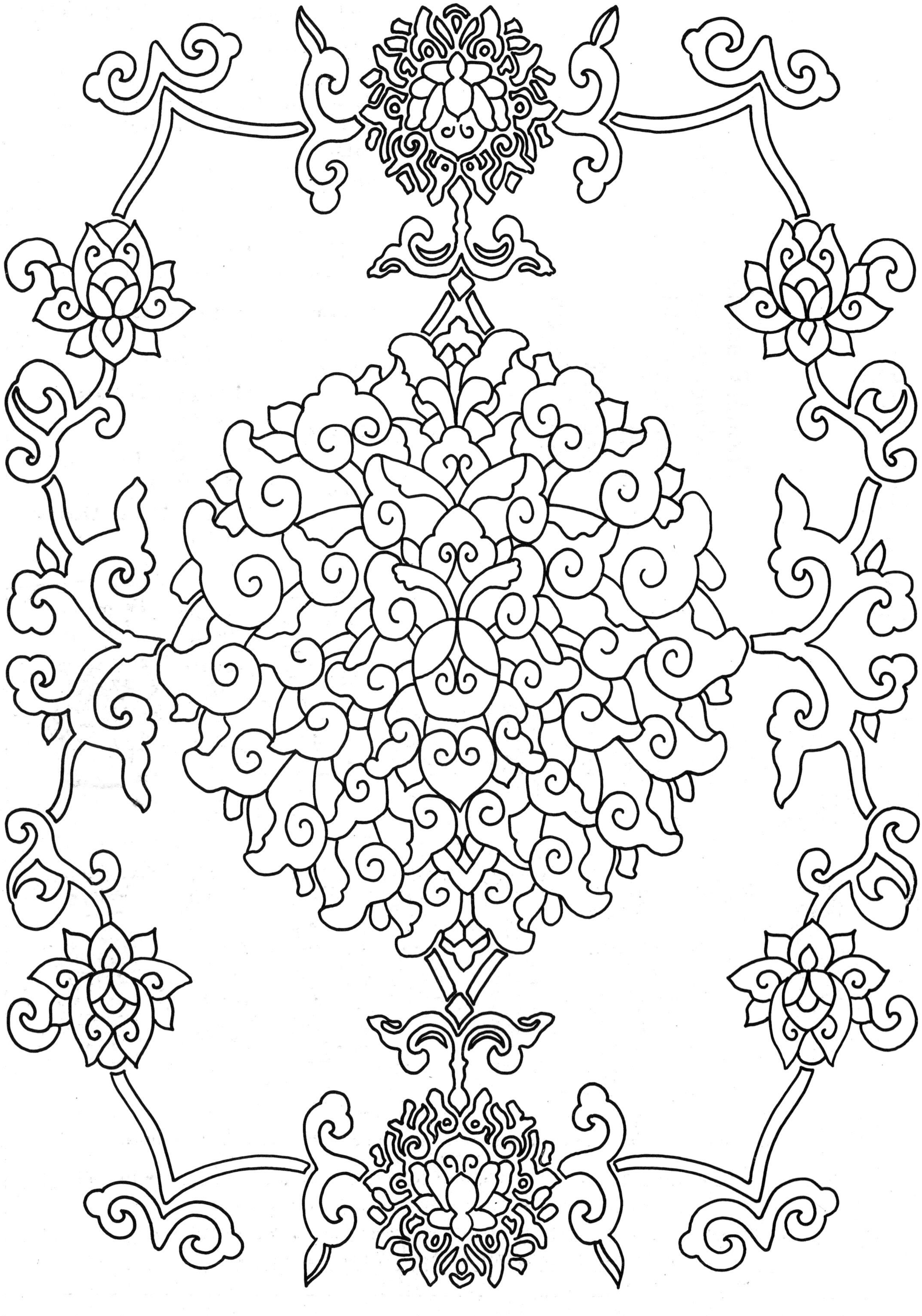